Arab Digital Journalism

Responding to urgent calls to de-westernise Media and Journalism Studies and shed light on local agencies, this book examines digital journalistic practices in the Arab region, exploring how Arab journalists understand their roles and how digital technologies in Arab newsrooms are used to influence public opinion.

Drawing on dozens of articles penned by Arab media professionals and scholars, supplemented with informal conversations with journalists, this book reviews the historical development of digital journalism in the region and individual journalists' perceptions of this development. While technology has provided a new platform for citizens and powerful agents to exchange views, this text examines how it has simultaneously allowed Arab states and authorities to conduct surveillance on journalists, curtail the rise of citizen journalism, and maintain offline hierarchal forms of political, economic, and cultural powers. Mellor also explores how digital technology serves to cement Western hegemony of the information world order, with Arab media organisations and audiences judged to be mere recipients, rather than producers, of such information.

Arab Digital Journalism offers an important contribution to the emerging field of digital journalism in the Global South and is a valuable resource for students and researchers interested in media, journalism, communication, and development studies.

Noha Mellor is Professor of Media at the University of Sharjah, UAE. She is also a Visiting Professor at Bournemouth University, UK.

Disruptions
Studies in Digital Journalism
Series editor: Bob Franklin

Disruptions refers to the radical changes provoked by the affordances of digital technologies that occur at a pace and on a scale that disrupts settled understandings and traditional ways of creating value, interacting and communicating both socially and professionally. The consequences for digital journalism involve far-reaching changes to business models, professional practices, roles, ethics, products and even challenges to the accepted definitions and understandings of journalism. For Digital Journalism Studies, the field of academic inquiry which explores and examines digital journalism, disruption results in paradigmatic and tectonic shifts in scholarly concerns. It prompts reconsideration of research methods, theoretical analyses and responses (oppositional and consensual) to such changes, which have been described as being akin to 'a moment of mind-blowing uncertainty'.

Routledge's book series *Disruptions: Studies in Digital Journalism* seeks to capture, examine and analyse these moments of exciting and explosive professional and scholarly innovation which characterise developments in the day-to-day practice of journalism in an age of digital media, and which are articulated in the newly emerging academic discipline of Digital Journalism Studies.

Arab Digital Journalism
Noha Mellor

News Journalism and Twitter
Disruption, Adaption and Normalisation
Chrysi Dagoula

Digital Journalism and the Facilitation of Hate
Gregory P. Perreault

For more information about this series, please visit: www.routledge.com/Disruptions/book-series/DISRUPTDIGJOUR

Arab Digital Journalism

Noha Mellor

LONDON AND NEW YORK

First published 2023
by Routledge
4 Park Square, Milton Park, Abingdon, Oxon OX14 4RN

and by Routledge
605 Third Avenue, New York, NY 10158

Routledge is an imprint of the Taylor & Francis Group, an informa business

© 2023 Noha Mellor

The right of Noha Mellor to be identified as author of this work has been asserted in accordance with sections 77 and 78 of the Copyright, Designs and Patents Act 1988.

All rights reserved. No part of this book may be reprinted or reproduced or utilised in any form or by any electronic, mechanical, or other means, now known or hereafter invented, including photocopying and recording, or in any information storage or retrieval system, without permission in writing from the publishers.

Trademark notice: Product or corporate names may be trademarks or registered trademarks, and are used only for identification and explanation without intent to infringe.

British Library Cataloguing-in-Publication Data
A catalogue record for this book is available from the British Library

ISBN: 9781032111971 (hbk)
ISBN: 9781032111988 (pbk)
ISBN: 9781003218838 (ebk)

DOI: 10.4324/9781003218838

Typeset in Times New Roman
by codeMantra

Contents

	List of figures and table	vii
	List of acronyms	ix
	Introduction: a tale of three regions	1
1	Infrastructure	16
2	Newsrooms	34
3	Journalists	53
4	Audiences	72
5	COVID-19	90
	Conclusion: two-tier journalism	111
	Index	127

List of figures and table

Figures

0.1	Arab youth unemployment in selected states	6
0.2	Mobile subscription per 100 inhabitants	8
0.3	Penetration of the internet compared to the population in selected Arab states	8
1.1	Productivity in percentages for every child born in selected states	20
2.1	The development of online and digital media in the Arab region	36
2.2	Web traffic for the three main pan-Arab news channels	42
5.1	Total press violations related to COVID-19 coverage	105

Table

5.1	Arab fact checking services	99

Acronyms

AMEJA	Arab and Middle Eastern Journalists Association
Arab DJN	Arab Data Journalism Network
AUC	African Union Commission
ESCWA	United Nations Economic and Social Commission for Western Asia
EY	Ernst & Young (company)
FB	Facebook
GCC	Gulf Cooperation Council
GDP	Gross Domestic Product
HCI	Human Capital Index
ICA	International Communication Association
ICIJ	International Consortium of Investigative Journalists
ICT	Information and Communications Technology
IFEX	International Freedom of Expression Exchange (network)
IJNET	Interntional Journalsits Network
ILO	International Labour Organization
IPI	International Press Institute
IPSOS	Institut Publique de Sondage d'Opinion Secteur
ITU	International Telecommunication Union
JWT (Intelligence)	J. Walter Thompson company
KFCRIS	King Faisal for Research and Islamic Studies
LCFP	Libyan Center for Freedom of Press
MBC	Middle East Broadcasting Corporation
MENA	Middle East and North Africa
OECD	Organization for Economic Co-operation and Development
OSN	Orbit Showtime Network

x *Acronyms*

OTT	Over-the-top media
PWC	PricewaterhouseCoopers (company)
ROI	Return on Investment
SDG	Sustainable Development Goals
UNDESA	United Nations Department of Economic and Social Affairs
UNDP	United Nations Development Programme
USAID	United States Agency for International Development
VOD	Video on Demand
VoIP	Voice over Internet Protocol

Introduction
A tale of three regions

In the wake of the 2011 Arab uprisings, American Big Tech companies were hailed as 'the ultimate arbiters on free speech online' and one driving force behind the uprisings (Guesmi, 2021). Authors such as Parag Khanna (2016) celebrated the growing globalisation of infrastructure and communications which brought about not only an increasing sense of connectivity but also prosperity. Ten years later, this depiction had changed with social media platforms now being accused of serving as platforms of misinformation in the region. Arab commentators have pointed to the lack of transparency concerning how such Big Tech companies make decisions about suspending accounts targeting the region and the vague algorithms that push certain content while concealing others. Those commentators have also argued that published reports by Big Tech which name and shame certain Arab sites as being sources of fake news, may only be a drop in the ocean compared to the true and 'unfathomable number of trolls and bots on Arab social media' (Guesmi, 2021). Another concern with the Big Tech companies is that they seize most of the digital advertising revenue to the detriment of Arab newsrooms.

There has been a burgeoning literature looking at the use of digital media in activism since 2011, but only a paucity of studies (in English) exist which have looked closely at digital journalism in the Arab region. This book fills this gap by examining digital journalism in the Arab region – a region that is characterised by similarities and differences, as well as stark contradictions. To understand the Arab digital media sphere, it is essential first to examine, albeit briefly, these similarities and differences, and their impact on the media sector.

One region or three regions?

The Arab region is home to more than 436 million people and includes 18 Arabic-speaking states: Algeria, Morocco, Tunisia, Libya, Egypt, Sudan, Jordan, Syria, Lebanon, Iraq, Yemen, Kuwait, Oman, Saudi

DOI: 10.4324/9781003218838-1

2 Introduction: a tale of three regions

Arabia, the United Arab Emirates, Qatar, Bahrain, and the Palestinian Authorities. Using the adjective 'Arab' to categorise the region creates the illusion of a region which consists of a homogeneous population defined as Arab; the truth, however, is that the word 'Arab' does not denote a specific ethnicity. Indeed, it may only refer to the shared written language or Modern Standard Arabic, while each state has its own vernacular or mother tongue. Heads of state usually dip into the narrative of 'Arabism' when it suits their goals while highlighting the differences with other Arab states in times of conflict. Individuals do the same and emphasise their Arab identity when it is advantageous to them. In truth, each state has been influenced by the ideas and ideologies of neighbouring countries. Egypt, for example, 'has been heavily shaped by the constructive and destructive forces of its region including Dubai-style capitalism, Tunisia's revolution, Moroccan Sufism, Saudi Wahabism, and Levant-authored pan-Arabism' (Ali, 2021).

The Arab states differ among themselves in terms of economic development, political structure, population size, and level of urbanisation – not to mention ethnic and religious diversity within each state. The region is roughly divided into three sub-regions. The Gulf Cooperation Council (GCC) states which comprise the oil-rich countries of Saudi Arabia, Kuwait, Bahrain, Qatar, Oman, and the UAE were formed in 1981 to cement their economic and political unity. This unity recently came under tension after Saudi Arabia, Bahrain, the UAE, and later Egypt decided to impose a blockade against Qatar in 2017 which ended in 2021. There is also the Maghreb sub-region which comprises Morocco, Algeria, Tunisia, and Libya. These states also attempted to form their own Arab Maghreb Union in 1989 (with Mauritania) but it is largely regarded as dormant because of disagreements, particularly between Algeria and Morocco. These came to a head after Algeria cut its diplomatic ties with Morocco in 2021. Finally, there is the Mashreq sub-region which comprises Jordan, Syria, Palestine, Lebanon, Egypt, and Iraq. Yemen and Sudan are sometimes grouped with the Gulf and Mashreq regions, respectively (Mellor, 2011, 104–5).

If divided according to population size, Egypt will be ranked at the top (with more than 100 million inhabitants) while Qatar will be placed at the bottom (with less than 3 million inhabitants of which 90 per cent are expatriates). If divided in terms of press history, then countries such as Lebanon, Egypt, Syria, and Iraq would be at the top, as they recorded the first periodicals in the region in contrast to the Gulf States whose press ventures emerged around the mid-20th century. The region can also be divided in terms of resources. The United Nations Development Programme (UNDP, 2020), for example, divides the region into

Introduction: a tale of three regions 3

three groups: oil-exporting countries (Algeria, Bahrain, Kuwait, Saudi Arabia, Oman, Qatar, and the UAE); oil-importing middle-income countries (Egypt, Jordan, Morocco, and Tunisia); and fragile and crisis countries (Iraq, Lebanon, Syria, Libya, Palestine, Sudan, and Yemen).

These socio-economic divisions have manifested themselves in failed attempts at media collaboration; for instance, Arab states' efforts to establish a joint Arab news agency to balance the dominance of Western agencies were unsuccessful. They disagreed on leadership and whether directors and the number of employees should be proportionate to the population (making Egypt the de facto leader), or whether leadership should be attached to financial resources, thus granting this role to Saudi Arabia as the richest state (Mellor, 2005, p. 44). The discussions eventually led to the establishment of the Federation of Arab News Agencies, headquartered in Lebanon, which includes 18 or 19 national news agencies as members (fananews.com).

Regional integration in terms of trade has also been difficult because of the cronyism between the states and economic elites, conflicts and violence in many states, and the lack of trust among Arab states. Examples of this mistrust include the strained relationship between Algeria and Morocco; the war in Yemen and the conflict in Syria, which has led to the blockade against Qatar by Saudi Arabia, Egypt, the UAE, and Bahrain; the banning of the Islamist movement and the Muslim Brotherhood in Saudi Arabia, the UAE, and Egypt which has further strained relations with Turkey and Qatar; and the conflict in Libya. Each conflict comes with an economic cost evaluated at 5 per cent of the value of trade within the region. The Syrian conflict, for one, not only had an impact on the trade volume in Syria but in several other countries in Mashreq (Arezki et al., 2020, p. 42).

The region also misses out on labour market integration strategies, although historically, the GCC states absorbed a large number of skilled workers from poorer states. During the past three decades, however, some GCC states have adopted various programmes aimed at nationalising their labour force, replacing (Arab) expatriates with Gulf nationals where possible. Saudi Arabia, for example, has been promoting 'Saudisation' schemes to ensure Saudis get better opportunities in the labour market including in the media industries. The Saudi government introduced the In-Kingdom Total Value Add (IKTVA) scheme in December 2015, to localise labour and services. Other GCC states introduced similar schemes such as the 'Omanisation' programme in Oman to replace expatriate manpower with Omani personnel to prepare them to take over jobs currently held by over 1.6 million expatriates (Hasan & Blackwell, 2015). Such schemes will inevitably reduce the

4 Introduction: a tale of three regions

number of Arab nationals who have been working in the GCC states for years, and consequently also reduce the remittances they send back to their home countries which form an integral part of the national GDP of those countries. The UAE, on the other hand, has announced that it will grant citizenship to foreigners nominated by the royals, while Qatar announced that it would grant permanent residence to foreign talents, in acknowledgement of the consistent need for skills that are not currently available in the region, especially in the field of digital technology.

In addition to sharing the written Arabic language, Arab States share the fact that their fate was shaped by the inter-War period (1918–1939). This region is still experiencing issues which stemmed from that era (Kamrava, 2013). The Arab world emerged at the end of the Ottoman Empire when former European colonial powers divided the region into smaller protectorates. The Sykes-Picot agreement, for example, allocated what is today Israel, Palestine, Jordan, and Southern Iraq to Britain, while Syria, Lebanon, and Northern Iraq were allocated to France. The porous borders resulted in several inter-regional territorial disputes, some of which were settled, while others are still ongoing. Another enduring consequence of colonialism is that it made ethnic and religious divisions 'seem natural, historical, and timeless to the respective populations' (Ali, 2021).

The notion of citizenship also has unique connotations in the Arab region, with differentiated forms of citizenship across the region. Formerly colonised countries such as Algeria and Egypt, for example, had to fight for their national citizenship, and negotiate their sovereignty with former colonial powers (France and Britain respectively), whereas newly emerged states such as Jordan (established in 1946), Lebanon (1943), Syria (1946), and Iraq (1932) had to craft their own national identity following the formation of their states in the first half of the 20th century. The GCC states have adopted a form of citizenship that is based on tribal and familial affiliation following the formation of their states: Saudi Arabia (1932), Kuwait (1961), Qatar (1971), the UAE (1971), and Oman (1951). Palestine is another unique case in which Palestinians are differentiated according to their residence: those in Israel versus those in the West Bank and Gaza. These different grades of citizenship consequently exist in several countries by privileging some citizens over others (Abdellatif, Pagliani & Hsu, 2019, pp. 4–5). To strengthen the concepts of citizenship and national identity, Arab states use highly politicised educational curricula to differentiate their history and identity from neighbouring states. Following the independence of all Arab territories between the 1930s and the 1970s, each Arab state declared a new national identity, a flag, and, for many states, a new constitution. Identity politics is therefore pivotal in

Introduction: a tale of three regions 5

understanding the region and its media landscape, as it informs each state's conception of its interests.

The various chapters illustrate the manifestation of the socio-economic differences in the increasing digital divide among the Arab states, cyber rivalry, and how the increasing youth demographics have all shaped the digital media sphere.

The youth 'bulge'

Arab youth between the ages of 15 and 29 represent the majority of the population in the region. This segment (under the age of 30) forms nearly 70 per cent of the population in Saudi Arabia, 50 per cent in the UAE, and 60 per cent in Egypt. Thanks to increasing internet penetration rates, young audiences have taken to new and social media platforms to seek, and sometimes create new content. The Internet penetration in Saudi Arabia is 93 per cent for instance, and mobile phone penetration is 115 per cent; Saudi Arabia also has 9 per cent of the world's *Snapchat* users and leads the region in *Instagram* and *Twitter* accounts. It also leads the world in per capita social media users who access video content online. In Jordan, 90 per cent or more of the population is covered by the 4G network, and the majority of internet users are younger people aged 18–35 years. Between 2012 and 2018, Jordanians' media consumption shifted towards digital media, with internet use rising from 23 per cent in 2012 to 88 per cent in 2018, whereas television viewing fell from 93 to 80 per cent, and the daily press from 18 to 6 per cent during the same period (USAID, 2020, p. 1).

The high proportion of the youthful population has created a so-called 'youth bulge' as well as the securitisation of youth as one of the main sources of instability; the 2011 uprisings, however, have provided a different narrative of Arab youth as the driver of development and democracy (Murphy, 2018). With the increasing digital literacy of Arab youth under 24, who form 50 per cent of the region's population, digital media consumption and production across the region are notably high, particularly in well-connected societies such as the GCC states (Dubai Press Club, 2018). The rate of connectivity is highest in Saudi Arabia, which is *YouTube*'s largest market worldwide in terms of per capita consumption. Arab youth are avid consumers of social media. Libya, the UAE, and Qatar have the highest reach for *Facebook* (100 per cent, 93 per cent, and 90 per cent respectively), and Egypt is the 9th largest market for *Facebook* in the region in terms of users (44 million users), while *Snapchat* reaches 67 million users in the region each month, including 90 per cent of young people under the age of 34 in Saudi Arabia (Radcliffe & Abuhmaid, 2021). *WhatsApp* is heavily used across several

Arab states, such as Saudi Arabia where one Travel Agency, *Almosafer*, recorded more than 2,000 *WhatsApp* conversations a day in early 2020. The use of this app increased significantly during the COVID-19 lockdowns to communicate messages to citizens, and to answer the most common questions. This led to Saudi Arabia pondering the development of local messaging services like *WhatsApp* to reduce its reliance on the American messaging service (Radcliffe & Abuhmaid, 2021).

Despite the high rate of internet penetration in the region, particularly in the oil-rich countries, the whole region records a lower Human Capital Index compared to countries of comparable levels of income, and the quality of school education is low, despite the high literacy rate. The problem is exacerbated when young people enrol in higher educational institutions, obtaining knowledge and skills that do not match the needs of the labour market (El-Saharty et al., 2020, p. 18). The region has consequently been faced with poor learning outcomes, a marked discrepancy between the skills of recent graduates and the needs of the labour market, as well as a huge gap in wages between the public and private sectors. These factors discourage young people from pursuing jobs in the private sector or self-employment (El-Saharty et al., 2020). Overall, the average youth unemployment rate across the region is 25 per cent – the highest in the world – coupled with the modest female labour force participation of 20 per cent (World Bank, 2019).

Figure 0.1 Arab youth unemployment in selected states
Source: *World Bank*, 2021.

Introduction: a tale of three regions 7

Digital labour, on the other hand, is acutely needed (see Chapter 1), in order to deal with the increasing record of global cyber-attacks. There were more than 1,200 breaches of data worldwide in Novemeber 2019 alone, with the highest number in the banking and healthcare sectors in the USA followed by the Middle East. The record is expected to grow in the coming years, driven by the increasing cloud migration, and *Internet of Things* (IoT) devices (Cisco, 2020, p. 21). Chapters 2 and 3 expand on this discussion of the acute need for digital labour, particularly in the media sphere, and the GCC states' efforts to train their native citizens as well as to attract digital labour from neighbouring, poorer, countries.

Digital divide

The digital sphere has exacerbated inequalities among Arab states, divided between those in the oil-rich and well-connected countries versus citizens in less advantaged states, as well as refugees who are deprived of adequate and reliable access to the Internet. Unreliable connections have worsened during COVID-19 with considerable pressure added to those connections reflecting the increasing demand for video conferencing and other digital services.

The region is divided broadly into two blocs in terms of digital capabilities: the first bloc includes states with a high record of mobile subscriptions, or well above the regional average of 99 mobile subscriptions per 100 inhabitants. These include the oil-rich Gulf States as well as Syria, Algeria, and Morocco. The second bloc includes countries with a below-average record: Egypt (95), Iraq (95), Libya (91), Palestine (86), Sudan (77), Jordan (77), Lebanon (62), and Yemen (54). Egypt is still regarded as the host of the largest telecommunication sector in the region due to its high population (more than 100 million inhabitants).

Mobile connectivity is expected to expand further in the next year. By 2023, the number of internet users in the Middle East and North Africa (MENA) region is expected to grow by 9 per cent while mobile users will grow by a further 4 per cent (Cisco, 2020, p. 4).

Internet access is not always evenly available across the region, regardless of mobile coverage, given the stark socio-economic differences among Arab states and the high cost of accessing data online. The cost of accessing only 1GB of data, for instance, is roughly 5 per cent of monthly income (*ITU*, 2021, p. 8). The cost of 1GB of data is US$15 in a poor country such as Yemen, where GDP per capita is circa US$720, whereas it costs US$12 in Qatar where the GPD per capita is circa US$50,800; the cost for the same service is US$2 in both Bahrain and Kuwait (*Capital.co.uk*, 2021).

8 *Introduction: a tale of three regions*

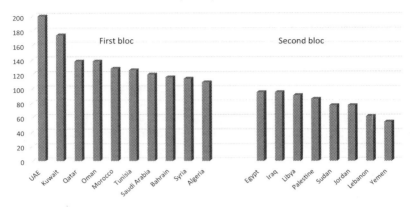

Figure 0.2 Mobile subscription per 100 inhabitants
Source: *International Telecommunication Union – (ITU*, 2021, p. 6).

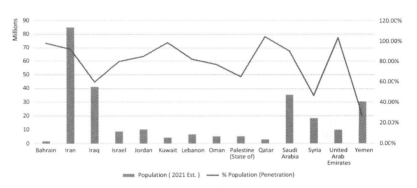

Figure 0.3 Penetration of the internet compared to the population in selected Arab states
Source: https://www.internetworldstats.com/

Internet connectivity also varies from one state to another with some GCC states having over 100 per cent connectivity while Yemen has the lowest penetration rate of 26 per cent.

The Arab states, moreover, have been focusing their investments on the telecommunications market, which plays a pivotal role in securing the affordability and availability of internet connections to digital users and content producers. Generally, the region has seen continuing, albeit slow, growth in the Information and Communications Technology (ICT) sector in terms of infrastructure, access, and use,

Introduction: a tale of three regions 9

with the spending on Artificial Intelligence (AI) systems in the region estimated to be circa US$ 374 million in 2020 (*ITU*, 2021, p. 4). The adoption of AI is led mainly by the UAE, Saudi Arabia, and Qatar, even though most companies in the region feel they are not using AI in an advanced way due to a lack of digital talents and training (*ITU*, 2021, p. 23). In newsrooms, AI arguably provides tools for the automatic summarisation of information and automation of recurring reports such as sports and stock market news. However, such AI tools are usually developed in the English language (as will be discussed in the subsequent chapters), and, unless Arabic-language versions are available, they may not be accessible to many Arab newsrooms. The problem is exacerbated by two more factors: the lack of digital talents in the Arab region, coupled with the unwillingness of some Big Tech companies (such as *Facebook*) to develop digital tools in the Arabic language since half of their revenue is generated in North America. This is why there is a need for targeted educational programmes even though the young Arab generation is more tech-savvy and globally orientated than previous ones. This new generation still needs to be equipped with the knowledge required to develop new applications in Arabic.

Liberating technology?

The Arab region is considered to be part of the so-called 'Global South' – the new term replacing old classifications such as Third World and Developing World. The term is used in this book as a referent to a post-colonial region with unique social, cultural, and political legacies which inevitably make the region dependent on Western powers, particularly the USA and Europe. This form of dependency is manifested in all domains: military armament, economic development, political interests, and, most relevant to this book, technological development. The region is also dependent on Western intellectual thought, with all Arab universities adopting Western theories – often without much critical reflection – as the guiding concepts to understand the world.

The following chapters demonstrate that digital technology is not levelling the field. While it has provided a new platform for ordinary citizens as well as powerful agents to exchange views, the digital sphere has maintained the offline hierarchal forms of political, economic, and even cultural powers. The largest share of activities and resources are still performed by the powerful minority, while the vast majority are mere recipients and followers of the minority. Consequently, the digital sphere reproduces the same offline power relations.

10 Introduction: a tale of three regions

Western literature about digital journalism tends to focus on four functions or themes, namely, the participatory nature of digital media, the undermining of traditional gatekeepers' power, the innovative character of digital media, and the rise of entrepreneurial journalists or those who can 'raise their own funding, and brand themselves in the social media era' (Kreiss & Brenne, 2016, p. 299). Arabic literature, on the other hand, tends to highlight themes of the ubiquity of digital technology, particularly social media platforms, as a source of information and newsgathering for both audiences and journalists, while relegating the participatory theme and the journalists' entrepreneurship. The Arab studies surveyed in this book also do not touch on the hegemony of Western technology in terms of the dominance of Big Tech in digital advertising, although Arab journalists (Chapters 2 and 3) point to this dominance as one cause of the deterioration of the printed press as well as news values, now focusing mainly on infotainment to get more 'clicks'.

Western studies and commentaries about the Arab region tend to depict power as a causal relation between an all-powerful state and subordinate citizens, focusing on the role of politics in the media sphere. Such analyses usually focus on the role of (authoritarian) states in the journalism field, while bracketing the role of journalists and audiences as active agents. This book shows that such an unbalanced focus on the role of the state has not provided a nuanced understanding of the Arab media sector which has flourished, rather than shrunk, since the 1990s. There is a need to expand the analysis of power relations which are not limited to the state level but should be seen through interstate rivalries as well as the position of Arab countries within the global economy.

Finally, digital technology has disrupted traditional media business models in the region which depended solely on media advertising revenues from public and private clients. Digital technology has enabled new entrants to the field of Arab digital news, including news aggregators such as the Egyptian *Akhbarak.net*. It is thus not only 'affluent media users in the high-income democracies [that] have access to more content from more sources, and often for free', as Nielsen (2016, 63) argues. In fact, Arab media users today, especially in high-income countries such as the GCC states, have access to far more sources than those available to Western users. It is enough to mention that the number of satellite channels well exceeds 1,300 (as of 2016), and the amount of amateur content has massively increased over the past few years, including content created by those in the diaspora communities. In this saturated market, Arab news outlets, whether legacy or natively

Introduction: a tale of three regions 11

digital, are facing huge financial pressure in a market dominated by digital entertainment media, particularly *Netflix,* and now the Saudi-owned *Shahid,* and a digital advertising market that is largely monopolised by the Big Tech companies.

Tracing the 'disruption' in Arab journalism

The analysis in the subsequent chapters is based on different forms of evidence, including more than 80 documents ranging from opinion pieces penned by Arab journalists, in which they reflect on their experiences in the digital sphere to scholarly articles and books by Arab scholars, in addition to Arabic and English language reports from regional and international organisations about the digital development in the Arab region. I have supplemented this data with ten informal conversations with Arab journalists based in Dubai and London. This evidence base reflects Arab journalists' and scholars' voices which ultimately create a narrative path for the readers to navigate. The focus of these selected pieces of evidence is on the impact of digital technology on the media sphere and particularly on journalistic practices.

These pieces of evidence provide documentary data and broad case studies of the uses of digital technology in the Arab journalism field. The aim is to establish the extent of 'disruption' caused by digital technology through a form of 'process tracing' of these cases (Beach & Pedersen, 2013), in terms of business models and the shift to digital advertising, but also changing news values, especially with the rise of citizen journalism, which, theoretically at least, has undermined the power of journalists as traditional gatekeepers. But also the extent of engagement with audiences, particularly young people who constitute the majority of Arab populations. The examples drawn upon in the subsequent chapters shed light on both the micro- and macro-levels of journalistic practices, namely, the impact of investment in digital infrastructure, investment in setting up new digital outlets, the digital presence of legacy media, and the adoption of this technology by individual journalists who have found a new platform on the Internet for entrepreneurial and alternative news business.

The aim is to facilitate a space for Arab *voices*, whether practitioners or scholars. Voice here is defined as the expression of Arab views and opinions, although I realise the presence of a hierarchy of voices (Couldry, 2010) where some voices (particularly Western voices) are more authoritative than Arab ones since Western practitioners and scholars have generally amassed a higher symbolic power within the journalism field than their Arab counterparts. I also acknowledge

12   *Introduction: a tale of three regions*

that Arab journalists do not always speak from a single position (Esin, Fathi & Squire, 2014, pp. 205–6) but draw on other discourses such as those related to nationalism, politics, international relations, and the position of the Arab World within the global sphere.

As a researcher, I position myself as a 'supportive voice' (Esin, Fathi & Squire, 2014, p. 209) that facilitates Arab journalists' and scholars' views as part of the global journalism field. As I see it, my personal and professional background (as a native Egyptian and former journalist) has given me a unique opportunity to access indigenous perspectives, which are different from those offered by Western scholars. I, therefore, emphasise the need to draw on Arabic-language sources in order to engage with more native voices rather than interpreting the media and journalism field solely from pervasive Eurocentric perspectives. That said, I also realise the hierarchy of voices within Western media scholarship creating a two-tier media scholarship (more on this in the Conclusion chapter).

The following discussion will focus on examples of national and pan-Arab newsrooms but will exclude Western-subsided outlets such as *BBC Arabic* (London), *al-Hurra* (Washington DC), *France 24 Arabic* (Paris), *Deutsche Welle Arabic* (Berlin), Russia's *RT Arabic* (Moscow), as well as the Arabic service of *China Global Network* (Beijing). Although the journalists working in those foreign outlets constitute a 'cosmopolitan cohort' who move from one job to another across national and pan-Arab newsrooms (see Mellor, 2011), the Western-subsidised outlets have been excluded because they belong to a different news culture, and they have access to resources unavailable to other local and regional outlets.

Outline of the book

The following chapters focus on Arab digital journalism defined as the process of gathering, curating, and storytelling the news for the interest of the general public, while the news is defined as informative content characterised by its relevance, timeliness, and impact on users. Digital journalism here refers to news content created for use on the Internet, but it also refers to the 'online press' introduced in the 1990s by many pan-Arab outlets, as well as the natively digital outlets emerging, particularly post-2011 (Chapter 2).

The analysis of the Arab media field must take into account the pivotal role of Arab diaspora communities. North Africa and West Asia, in fact, host nearly 50 million migrants, of which 29 million were added between 2000 and 2020, and 9 million of them were refugees

Introduction: a tale of three regions   13

(UNDESA, 2020, p. 8). It was around 38 per cent of the total migration in the world in 2020 which originated from North Africa and Western Asia, particularly from Syria and Afghanistan. Syrian displaced persons constituted around one-fifth or 6.7 million of international migrants in 2020, followed by Palestine with circa 5.7 million (UNDESA, 2020, pp. 9–17). For professional displaced journalists residing within the region, there may be some opportunities to join the pan-Arab newsrooms such as *Al-Jazeera* or *Al-Arabiya*, while budding journalists have joined the numerous stations set up by Syrian refugees in Turkey, mostly funded by Qatar and Turkey. For those refugees who have moved to Europe, however, there have been fewer opportunities to set up news websites, serving as information fora for other refugees (Chapters 3 and 4).

The shift to digital platforms has also resulted in an increasing focus on audience analytics and metrics, and an increasing reliance on digital advertising for revenue (Steensen & Westlund, 2021, p. 4). When it comes to audience metrics, Arab newsrooms have depended mostly on the Big Tech companies such as *Facebook* and *Twitter* to offer solutions based on the number of impressions, clicks, and attention analytics (Chapter 4). This is also explained in Chapter 2 which demonstrates the unfair battle for digital advertising revenue, largely seized by the American Big Tech companies.

The impact of digital technology on journalistic practices, moreover, can be seen in the change in traditional news values, newsgathering, access to information and sources, as well as offering new opportunities for journalists and budding journalists, to enter the field as 'news entrepreneurs' as will be seen in Chapter 3. The digital media sphere also abounds with examples of false information, on the other hand, which was particularly noted during the peak of the COVID-19 pandemic in 2020, as discussed in Chapter 5.

To summarise, the following chapters demonstrate how digital technology has shaped the news ecosystem in the region, with the emergence of new forms of news and information distribution and sharing across digital platforms. The discussion begins with a focus on the digital infrastructure in the region and the increase in surveillance (Chapter 1). This is followed by a review of the digital journalistic practices beginning with the online press (Chapter 2), and a discussion about how the role of journalists has changed over time (Chapter 3). Chapter 4 sheds light on the way audiences embrace the new digital media, both as consumers and as producers of digital content, while Chapter 5 discusses how the global pandemic contributed to the further disruption and transformation of the digital media sphere. The Conclusion

14 *Introduction: a tale of three regions*

revisits the thesis of liberating technology and reflects on whether digital technology has widened or narrowed the existing digital divide in the journalism field – both regionally and globally.

References

Abdellatif, Adel, Paola Pagliani & Ellen Hsu (2019) Arab Human Development Report. Research Paper: Leaving No One Behind - Towards Inclusive Citizenship in Arab Countries. NY: UNDP.

Ali, Amro (2021) Unpacking the Arab Part of Identity, Spring, and World, MED Dialogue Series, no. 35, Konrad Adenauer Stiftung, February 2021.

Arezki, Rabah, Blanca Moreno-Dodson, Rachel Yuting Fan, Romeo Gansey, Ha Nguyen, Minh Cong Nguyen, Lili Mottaghi, Constantin Tsakas & Christina A. Wood. 2020. "Trading Together: Reviving the Middle East and North Africa Regional Integration in the Post-Covid Era" the Middle East and North Africa Economic Update (October). Washington, DC: World Bank. DOI: 10.1596/978-1-4648-1639-0

Beach, Derek & Rasmus Brun Pedersen (2013) *Process-Tracing Methods. Foundations and Guidelines.* Ann Arbor, MI: The University of Chicago Press.

Capital.co.uk (2021) The Cost of 1GB of Mobile Data in 230 Countries, https://www.cable.co.uk/mobiles/worldwide-data-pricing/#highlights

Cisco (2020) Annual Internet Report (2018–2023), CISCO, https://www.cisco.com/c/en/us/solutions/collateral/executive-perspectives/annual-internet-report/white-paper-c11-741490.html

Couldry, Nick (2010) *Why Voice Matters: Culture and Politics after Neoliberalism.* London: Sage.

Dubai Press Club. (2018). Arab Media Outlook 2016–2018: Youth…Content… Digital Media. Dubai, 5th Edition.

El-Saharty, Sameh, Igor Kheyfets, Christopher H. Herbst & Mohamed Ihsan Ajwad (2020). *Fostering Human Capital in the Gulf Cooperation Council Countries. International Development in Focus.* Washington, DC: World Bank. DOI:10.1596/978-1-4648-1582-9.

Esin, Cigdem, Mastoureh Fathi & Corinne Squire (2014) Narrative Analysis: The Constructionist Approach, in Uwe Flick (ed.) *The SAGE Handbook of Qualitative Data Analysis*, London: Sage, pp. 203–16.

Guesmi, Haythem (2021) The Social Media Myth about the Arab Spring. *Al-Jazeera*, January 27, 2021, https://www.aljazeera.com/opinions/2021/1/27/the-social-media-myth-about-the-arab-spring

Hasan, Deeba & Matt Blackwell (2015) Is Omanisation Working? https://www.y-oman.com/2015/08/omanisation-the-cost-of-control/ 19 August 2015

ITU (2021) *Digital Trends in the Arab States Region. Information and Communication Technology Trends and Developments in the Arab States Region, 2017–2020.* Geneva: International Telecommunication Union.

Introduction: a tale of three regions 15

Kamrava, Mehran (2013) *The Modern Middle East: A Political History since the First World War*, 3rd ed. California: University of California Press.

Khanna, Parag (2016) *Connectography: Mapping the Future of Global Civilization*. New York: Random House Inc.

Kreiss, Daniel & J Scott Brenne (2016) Normative Models of Digital Journalism, in Tamara Witschge, C.W. Anderson, David Domingo & Alfred Hermida (eds.) *The SAGE Handbook of Digital Journalism*. London: Sage, pp. 299–314.

Mellor, Noha (2005) *The Making of Arab News*. Lanham, MD: Rowman & Littlefield.

Mellor, Noha (2011) *Arab Journalists in pan-Arab Media*. New York: Hampton Press.

Murphy, Emma (2018) The In-Securitisation of Youth in the South and East Mediterranean. *The International Spectator*, Vol. 53(2), pp. 21–37.

Nielsen, Rasmus Kleis (2016) The Business of news, in Tamara Witschge, C.W. Anderson, David Domingo & Alfred Hermida (eds.) *The SAGE Handbook of Digital Journalism*. London: Sage, pp. 51–76.

Radcliffe, Damian & Handil Abuhmaid (2021) How the Middle East Used Social Media in 2020. *New Media Academy*, https://papers.ssrn.com/sol3/papers.cfm?abstract_id=3826011

Steensen, Steen & Oscar Westlund (2021) *What Is Digital Journalism Studies?* London: Routledge.

UNDESA (2020). International Migration 2020 Highlights, United Nations Department of Economic and Social Affairs, Population Division (ST/ESA/SER.A/452).

UNDP (2020) Compounding Crises. Will COVID-19 and Lower Oil Prices Lead to a New Development Paradigm in the Arab Region? NY: UNDP.

USAID (2020) Jordan Media Assessment, June 9, 2020, https://pdf.usaid.gov/pdf_docs/PA00WQVH.pdf

World Bank (2019) The Middle East and North Africa Human Capital Plan. Human Capital Project, https://thedocs.worldbank.org/en/doc/907071571420642349-0280022019/original/HCPMiddleEastPlanOct19.pdf

1 Infrastructure

To understand the digital media infrastructure in the Arab region, it is necessary to understand the digital readiness of the Arab economies which vary by sector. So far, the focus of Arab states has been on the financial sector and mobile telephony, while other sectors such as media and entertainment are far less ready (League of Arab States, 2020, p. 54). While the global digital economy is largely dominated by the USA and China (Herbert & Loudon, 2020), the digital economy represents only 10 per cent of the GDP of developing countries. The Arab digital economy, therefore, continues to exhibit the same (offline) dependency on US economic hegemony and American neoliberalism. The Arab region still needs to develop its capacity and capabilities to develop cloud computing and relevant applications, and generally must improve its digital infrastructure. It also needs to agree on unified tax rates for data services as well as regulations on global data service providers operating in the region (Ismail, 2021).

This chapter provides an overview of the key challenges facing Arab digital infrastructure. This chapter starts with a commentary on the governance of the Internet, which is largely dominated by the USA, despite the claims of American politicians that the Internet forms a new liberating digital sphere. This is followed by an explanation of the Arab states' focus on the telecommunications sector, highlighting the lack of human capital to lead the digital economy in the region. The focus on inter-state rivalries in cyberspace provides several examples of state-sponsored and non-state actors' cyber-attacks as a means of weakening their competitors. This rivalry is a key factor in understanding many online media projects that are used as new cyber tools against neighbouring countries. This chapter ends with highlights of the two forms of surveillance, namely, top-down surveillance and mundane surveillance.

DOI: 10.4324/9781003218838-2

Internet governance

Cyberspace is not an uncontrolled virtual notion but a system or network which is very much under the control of a few countries. State leaders such as former President Obama propagated the myth that the Internet represents a 'Wild West' scenario to distract from the fact that the Internet is actually based on physical infrastructure, mostly under the control of the US government and companies (Mainwaring, 2020, p. 219). It is no secret that the Internet is run by hundreds of undersea fibre optic cables connecting the world's regions, largely owned by US companies. These cables can be cut, exposing the whole world to the risk of an abrupt shutdown of all digital operations. For instance, three men were reported to have attempted to cut the undersea cable off the coast of Alexandria city, and, although they were caught by the Egyptian military, the operation was said to have caused a 60 per cent drop in Internet speed. Damage to one country such as Egypt is likely to affect other countries, too; also, in 2013, a ship's anchor damaged six cables off the coast of Alexandria which caused outages in many African countries (Chang, 2013).

Moreover, Internet governance has become a contentious political issue as it puts pressure on the states in the Global South in terms of regulating such borderless communication or handling massive amounts of data in the same way as Western countries can do. Decisions about digital standards and Internet architecture, moreover, are taken by states and corporations in the Global North. The debate about Internet governance, therefore, masks the divide among nations; even the choice of the term 'governance' is misleading as it denotes a form of coordination among sovereign, independent countries 'in the absence of overarching political authority' (Mueller, 2010, p. 8). Digital technology tends to be represented as a tool and a resource that can mobilise citizens to demand new reforms or policies while overlooking the fact that this technology is itself a target of political action (Mueller, 2010, p. 12). To develop inclusive governance rules of digital technology, there is therefore a need to develop a new framework that embeds classical liberal rights and helps to 'define, defend, and institutionalize individual rights and freedoms on a transnational scale' (Mueller, 2010, p. 271). Existing international initiatives such as the World Summit on Information Society or the Internet Governance Forum seem incapable of producing binding collective rules, and subsequently, the power to monitor the implementation of such rules.

While Western countries have enforced data protection laws, developing countries have lagged behind in implementing such regulations.

18 *Infrastructure*

This has left developing countries exposed to Western technological dominance by conducting large-scale data extraction and analysis and selling it for profit (Coleman, 2019). Thus, the control of the digital infrastructure has been in the hands of global corporations which extend previous control patterns in the offline sphere, while the less privileged have remained in the margins. The digital sphere is subjected to similar offline bureaucracy and has become another site illustrating the digital capabilities of countries such as surveillance technology; in this respect, the USA has become an information hegemon shaping the current infrastructure, data transactions, and algorithms, leaving behind smaller states, especially in the Global South, unable to catch up with this technology (Mainwaring, 2020, 227–31). The USA also has much power over cyberspace, with most of the .com and .net and .tv being generic domain names run by US firms, and therefore subject to US law enforcement.

Thus, the Arab states, as part of the Global South, are at the margins when it comes to shaping Internet policies. Obstacles to developing the Arab digital sector include data deprivation and an acute shortage of digital talent, as discussed below.

Scarce data

The digital media sector thrives on data, but data are rather a scarce commodity in the region. A survey among several Arab national statistics agencies, and a few national banks, showed that out of 47 per cent of work on big data projects, only 13 per cent of the projects were completed, while the rest lacked funding. More than half of the agencies stated that they did not use big data applications, citing the difficulties in accessing data regularly, not to mention the lack of skilled staff to handle these data (Lotfi, 2018). Data mining and data analytics are among the skills acutely needed in the region, which compels many agencies to seek collaboration with overseas partners to help upskill local staff (Lotfi, 2018, p. 6). Arab governments recently set up the Arab Development Portal (ADP) to serve as a knowledge resource with more than 8,300 indicators extracted from national and international sources and national statistics bureaux. Many of these sources are linked to the UN's SDG Tracking Tool (arabdevelopmentportal. com), although many inequality measures are based on household surveys which have not been conducted evenly across the whole region (Pagliani, 2020, p. 11).

The Arab region generally faces data deprivation and a lack of reliable statistical data which have had a negative impact on the

Infrastructure   19

effectiveness of governmental services (Pagliani, 2020, p. 2). In fact, the region performs worst in terms of the availability of data sources and accurate methodology, and this poses the challenge of conducting accurate international comparisons, not to mention the unreliability of available data to inform policymakers. The problem is especially acute in conflict-ridden countries such as Yemen, Syria, and Libya (Pagliani, 2020, p. 2). Reliable and accurate data is consequently not always publicly available in the region, partly because Arab statistics agencies have many weaknesses such as the lack of financial and human resources which contribute to the lack of reliable data.

Local hosting is another problem, as only 5 per cent of the content accessed in the region is hosted locally while the rest is hosted abroad. This makes it a more expensive solution (Internet Society, 2017, p. 22). Moreover, the Information and Communication Technology (ICT) sector in the region relies heavily on telecom and mobile services which offer most of the jobs. The mobile sector in North African countries, for example, employs around 390,000 people, and it indirectly creates another 650,000 jobs (AUC/OECD, 2021, p. 194). ICT services in Saudi Arabia account for 24 per cent of the operation in the digital sector, whereas telecom services account for 76 per cent of the market (ESCWA, 2017, p. 41). Overall, Arab exports of ICT represent less than 1 per cent of the global ICT goods trade, and less than 4 per cent of ICT services trade, focusing mainly on telecommunication services (ESCWA, 2017, p. 5).

The focus on telecom investment is often the reason behind Internet shutdowns or blockage of some services, and therefore shutdowns are not always due to political reasons. Governments tend to protect their telecommunication sector by blocking VoIP services such as *Skype* and *WhatsApp*, instead of encouraging or directing telecommunication providers to diversify their revenue (Internet Society, 2017, p. 13). States may also block access to the Internet at certain times. Algeria, for instance, blocks access to several social networks during high school examinations to curtail cheating attempts (Radcliffe & Abuhmaid, 2021, p. 27).

Another significant digital challenge facing the region is the lack of skilled talent, despite the region's increasing literacy rates, and the rising number of university graduates. This is discussed in the following section.

Stagnant human capital

According to the World Bank's Human Capital indicators for the MENA region, a child born in the region is likely to be 55 per cent productive by the age of 18, compared to 78 per cent of the potential

20 Infrastructure

for a child born in North America or the UK, 71 per cent in Europe and Central Asia, 61 per cent for East Asia and the Pacific (World Bank, 2019). There is a mix of chances and risks of reaching their potential in adulthood for every child born in the region today. If he or she was born in Algeria, for instance, he or she would likely be 53 per cent more productive in adulthood, provided that the child receives full education and health support. That percentage decreases to 52 for children born in Tunisia, and 50 per cent if born in Morocco. The chances further decline if they are born in Egypt (49 per cent), Iraq (41 per cent), Sudan (38 per cent), and Yemen (37 per cent). This percentage, however, increases if one is born in Jordan (55 per cent), Kuwait (56 per cent), West Bank and Gaza (58 per cent), peaking in the GCC states – the UAE (67 per cent), Bahrain (65 per cent), and Qatar (64 per cent).

Arab states' scores on the Human Capital Index (HCI) are lower than comparable states of the same level of income even in well-connected societies in the GCC states which have invested heavily in their telecommunication infrastructure. Human capital here is defined as the knowledge and skills accumulated throughout life. One main problem facing the region is the mismatch between graduates' skills and the needs of the labour market.

Although Arab states perform well in terms of the provision of education programmes, the quality of education has become a major concern, as it lags behind international averages. Teaching methods in particular are said to fail to stimulate critical thinking, relying heavily on memorisation (ESCWA, 2019). The whole region also suffers from

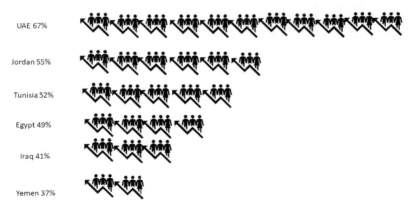

Figure 1.1 Productivity in percentages for every child born in selected states
Source: *World Bank* 2019.

Infrastructure 21

diploma inflation, since attaining credentials such as a university degree is more important than acquiring genuine skills and knowledge (ESCWA, 2019). Spending on education varies across the Arab region. Bahrain and Egypt each spends about 2.3 per cent of their GDP on education, while Jordan spends 3.6 per cent, Oman spends 5 per cent, and the West Bank and Gaza spends 5.3 per cent. The highest percentage is recorded in Tunisia (6.6 per cent in 2015). Not all Arab states have updated figures about their spending on education, but the regional average is estimated at 4.4 per cent (World Bank, 2019). The situation is exacerbated by the continuing conflicts in the region which has experienced wars throughout the 20th and 21st centuries (1948, 1967, and 1973 wars against Israel, civil war in Lebanon between 1975 and 1990, the Iraq-Iran wars 1981–88, the second Gulf War in 1991, Iraq War 2003, and post-2011 civil wars in Syria, Yemen, and Libya).

Moreover, Arab countries in North Africa urgently need to develop their human capital and accelerate the development of digital start-ups, currently unevenly distributed within the region. For instance, there were 92 start-ups in Egypt raising more than US$100,000 between 2011 and 2020, compared to only 3 in Algeria, 13 in Tunisia, and another 13 in Morocco during the same period (AUC/OECD, 2021, p. 195). The UAE, on the other hand, has developed a series of digital start-ups such as *DisruptAD* in Abu Dhabi, aiming to nurture over 1,000 start-ups over the coming five years, and link with global innovators (Magnitt, 2021). The UAE has also launched an 'Arab digital school' based on distance learning and is open to students from all over the world. The aim is to reach one million students by 2026 (thedigitalschool.org). The UAE also set up a ministry for Artificial Intelligence in 2017, and later expanded the ministry's portfolio to include Digital Economy and Remote Work Applications.

To compensate for the lack of local digital talent, the GCC states depend heavily on American labour to manage their digital ventures. To further boost its human capital in the ICT (and cybersecurity) sector, the GCC states also rely on the flow of expatriates from other Arab states such as Egypt, but this creates a problem for the exporting countries which find it hard to retain their local talent. The UAE most recently announced a new system of naturalisation, allowing dual nationality and granting UAE citizenship to highly skilled professionals (PWC, 2021). Other GCC states, however, have launched nationalisation strategies to reduce their dependency on foreign labour and replace it with nationals. It is still to be seen if these nationalisation and naturalisation plans would significantly reduce the current dependence on foreign labour.

22   *Infrastructure*

Finally, cyber-attacks constitute an imminent danger in the region, even though several Arab states have recently introduced cybersecurity strategies. These attacks are one of the dangers that can cripple its infrastructure with the private sector suffering frequent losses from such attacks (von Finckenstein, 2019, pp. 1–2). Cyber-attacks can happen as a result of denial of service to phishing, scams, and misinformation campaigns and can cost over half a US$billion to more than 50 per cent of the companies in the region. The problem is compounded by the regional skills gap, and the employers' reluctance to invest in cybersecurity training (von Finckenstein, 2019, p. 2).

Regional rivalry in cyberspace

The Arab states have realised the power of digital media and social networking platforms to boost their capabilities and compensate for their limited military power. There are some Arab states which have invested heavily in cyber-attacks and social media monitoring to help in their proxy wars and regional rivalries, although they have come to depend almost entirely on American technology and Western data scientists, due to the lack of digital talent in the region.

Arab state and non-state actors have run numerous 'hack and leak operations' such as the leaking of documents from the Saudi Ministry of Foreign Affairs by the Yemen Cyber Army in 2015. In the same year, the Saudi-funded newspaper *al-Hayat*, based in Lebanon, was hacked, and a picture of the *Hezbollah* leader was left on the website, with a message from the Yemen Cyber Army claiming its responsibility for this action (Shires, 2019, pp. 236–42). There were some cyber-attacks which were disguised as inauthentic news websites which promote political propaganda. The region has also seen a wave of leaks of key information. *Al-Jazeera*, for example, released classified documents relating to the Palestinian-Israeli negotiations – the Palestine Papers – in 2011, later shared with *The Guardian* in the UK. The documents were said to be leaked by an Arab source, and revealed the territorial concessions made by the Palestinian team; the content of those documents was later denied by Palestine, describing them as 'lies and half-truths' (Zayani, 2013, p. 25). Another example is the collaboration between *Al-Jazeera Arabic* and the Muslim Brotherhood media outlets, including *Mekameleen TV* in Turkey, to publish audio recordings of an alleged Egyptian security official instructing three journalists and an actress to help persuade the Egyptians of Trump's decision to move the American embassy to Jerusalem. The taped conversations opposed the official Egyptian position which rejected the American move (Emara, 2018). The leaks followed a report published by the *NY Times* correspondent in Cairo, David Kirkpatrick, in January 2018 (Kirkpatrick, 2018), in which he claimed he had obtained the recordings. The Egyptian media then attacked Kirkpatrick's account and raised doubts as to how the recordings reached *Al-Jazeera* and *Mekameleen TV*, alluding to the notion that Kirkpatrick may have a connection with those outlets.

In 2020, *Twitter* took down datasets attributed to actors in the region such as in Egypt where some accounts were linked to *El-Fagr* weekly newspaper; the same newspaper was named in a previous inauthentic activity takedown in 2019 (DiResta, Kheradpir & Miller, 2020). *Facebook* data centres, in addition, demonstrated that they had removed 31 *Facebook* accounts which contravened its terms and conditions in Egypt, Turkey, and Morocco, along with scores of *Instagram* accounts in the same countries associated with the Muslim Brotherhood movement, targeting Egypt, Libya, Tunisia, Yemen, and Saudi Arabia (*FB*, 2020). The suspended network seemed to have nearly 1.5 million followers on social media platforms, and they ran propaganda for Turkey and Qatar (where hundreds of the Egyptian members of the movement reside) and criticism of Saudi Arabia, Egypt, and the UAE, following their ban of the movement and subsequently imposing a blockade on Qatar. A study of these and other suspended accounts reveals that both sides (pro- and anti-Muslim Brotherhood) run similar campaigns by creating professional news pages, and sharing videos and information (Grossman, Fernanda Porras & Ramali, 2020).

A study of 16 states in the Middle East reveals the filtering mechanism practices by local governments to block content deemed hostile to their state interests. The blocked content was affiliated with various states and non-state actors (such as the *Houthis* in Yemen). Iran for example blocked certain content from Saudi Arabia and Bahrain, while Saudi Arabia blocked content affiliated with the *Houthis* in Yemen, Syria, and Iran; Syria, in turn, blocked content emanating from Saudi Arabia and UAE (Noman, 2019). In Egypt, the authorities closed 13 Shi'ite websites and TV channels, and some Sunni channels accused of inciting violence (*Al-Arab*, 2020 Feb. 26). Thus, states and non-state actors employ the digital sphere as a battleground to challenge the views of the opposition.

Moreover, Iraqi activists and journalists complain that they face threats and systematic defamation campaigns on social media by the so-called 'electronic armies' of loyalists to Iran who launch those campaigns using fake accounts. The electronic armies allegedly conduct their affairs in the offices of satellite channels in Iraq; technical

24 *Infrastructure*

experts affiliated with *Hezbollah* (based in Lebanon) have allegedly trained people at a military base in Baghdad (*Al-Hurra*, 2021). An investigation by the British newspaper, *The Telegraph* argues that *Hezbollah* has actively recruited and trained people from across the region to spread misinformation online (Crisp & al-Salhy, 2020). In Kuwait, information security calls for the government to invest in an electronic army, alleging that there are more than 50 Kuwaiti hackers who can join a new team to protect the government agencies in the country against cyber-attacks (Al-Hattab, 2020).

Consequently, the past few years have witnessed a proliferation of websites and social media sites that propagate, or conversely attack certain states' policies. Examples include *QatariLeaks*, expressing negative views of Qatar and its policies, *Othmanlly* (Ottoman), which is an Arabic-language *Facebook* page dedicated its activities to attacking Turkish policies, *Daqaeq.net* (Minutes) which is claimed to attack Qatari, Iranian and Turkish policies, *Khabayahom* (Their Secrets) producing content about the Muslim Brotherhood, as well as *al-Haqiqa* (Truth) and *al-Roya*, based in Mauritania (*Sasapost*, 2019). There is also a site called tasreeba.at, launched in 2018, but most of its activities were recorded in 2019 and 2020; it is not known who organises and funds this site. State institutions can also practice mutual surveillance. The Egyptian press (*Dostor*, 2014), for example, referred to the late President Morsi's speech in which he admitted taping calls between military leaders and the Supreme Election Committee to push for Morsi to step down.

State surveillance

It can be argued that while the new and social media platforms were initially hailed as liberating tools, they have been used as tools for oppression in places like the Middle East. Oppression, it is argued, can be exercised via surveillance of dissenting voices online, curtailing debates, blocking certain content, phishing and hacking, or manipulating public opinion by spreading false information and propaganda. Arab states still practice online surveillance, and forms of surveillance vary from hacking devices to spreading malware and extensively monitoring social media accounts to track dissidents (Hoffman, 2020). Egypt, for one, is claimed to target selected journalists, academics, lawyers, and activists through phishing and between 2016 and 2017, several Egyptian human rights activists and journalists were victims of phishing attacks (Hoffman, 2020). Some journalists even boast about their access to intelligence material including taped calls. For

Infrastructure 25

instance, one TV show in Egypt called '*Black Box*' was suspended in 2014 because it used to broadcast a range of taped phone calls by public figures including activists (Privacy International, 2019a). The Egyptian Supreme Media Council, however, decided in 2021 to impose sanctions on journalists who secretly recorded conversations and calls, without prior approval from the person being recorded. The Council justified the decision, citing the increase in cases of extortion in which some officials were allegedly threatened by journalists with the publication of their recordings if they did not meet the journalists' demands (Jamal, 2021a).

A former Egyptian telecommunication official denied that all phone calls were monitored as this was virtually impossible, with more than one billion minutes of calls made every hour, which would require expensive servers to store such massive data. No regime can block access to all proxy servers which a website uses because it is difficult to block all potential servers without interrupting the Internet service in one's own country (Al-Saqaf, 2016, p. 42). The Egyptian authorities, for one, cannot prevent users from accessing certain content, especially if it is accessed via proxy servers. It is not possible to shut down the entire Internet in Egypt without incurring massive economic losses. Syrian users similarly relied on a US-based proxy server to access blocked websites (Al-Saqaf, 2016, p. 45), but while states can aim to block some free telephony services (e.g., *Viber* and *WhatsApp*), they cannot possibly block all apps.

It can be argued that the idea of a handful of state officials that might control the digital sphere in the Middle East is implausible, as regimes do not have a monopoly on online information (Abrahams & Leber, 2021). Instead, some of the pro-regime information circulating online tends to be decentralised and stems from supporters – a bottom-up activity and not only a top-down manipulation. Examining hashtags supporting Saudi Arabia, for instance, did not rule out that many of those hashtags are organic 'cyber knights', and not the work of a centralised electronic army of bots (Abrahams & Leber, 2021, p. 1174). This argument is supported by the fact that Arab authoritarian regimes do not control social media platforms or the Internet, and their attempts to censor, hack, or restrict information are usually monitored by Western researchers.

Surveillance equipment is also usually purchased from European suppliers. In March 2018, it was revealed that the UK had sold surveillance equipment worth £70 million to several Arab states (Privacy International, 2019a). *Nokia Siemens* was accused of selling surveillance equipment to Bahrain to quash the protests in 2011, and of selling

26 *Infrastructure*

similar technology to Egypt. The German company *FinFisher* was claimed to have aided Bahrain to install spyware on dozens of computers of activists including the UK-based *Hassan Mushaima*; the UK company *BAE Systems* was said to conduct large-scale surveillance across the Middle East for Saudi Arabia, while the Israeli firm *NSO* is said to have sold the sophisticated surveillance platform *Pegasus* to several Arab countries (Hoffman, 2020). Between 2007 and 2011, Syria also purchased surveillance technology from Italy, France, Germany, and South Africa, and from Advanced German Technology, which sold similar equipment to the Libyan leader Gaddafi by using 'middlemen' companies (Privacy International, 2016). In Morocco, the government invested two million euros in the *Eagle* surveillance system in 2011, to monitor Internet traffic. The system was developed by a French company, which previously sold similar technology to the former Libyan leader, Gaddafi. Morocco also purchased similar surveillance technology from Swiss firms in 2013 and 2014, and the UK sold similar technology to six Arab states including Morocco (Privacy International, 2019b).

Mundane surveillance

While state surveillance has boomed in the Middle East, thanks to the availability of surveillance equipment in the Western market, what is more concerning is the mundane surveillance that has proliferated among ordinary citizens. Surveillance is no longer a top-down operation, managed solely by powerful states or corporations. Ordinary citizens can now target each other by using publicly available surveillance technology. Spying devices are commonly used among Arab couples to spy on one another, not only by tracing each other's phone calls but also via social media posts (Abu Hamour, 2018).[1] The Saudi authorities, for example, decided to penalise any person spying on his or her spouse with a hefty fine of up to nearly US$133,000. This decision also prompted the Egyptian *Mufti* to issue a *fatwa* (a legal ruling according to Shari'a) saying that spouses are not allowed, in Islam, to spy on one another as this is a breach of privacy (*Akhbar al-Youm*, 2019).

Spying devices have proliferated among ordinary citizens, and are being sold in the high streets in Cairo; a famous street called Abdel Aziz Street, nicknamed 'Spying Street', has become the hub for spying devices (*Dostor*, 2014). Shops casually sell spying devices ranging from tiny cameras and microphones hidden in shirt buttons, sunglasses, or pens, whose prices range from US$2 to US$700. Sellers admit that such devices are usually smuggled in electric devices or motorbike

Infrastructure 27

accessories, imported from Germany, the USA, Italy, China, and Japan (*Dostor*, 2014). Sellers also claim that buyers can be spouses using the devices to spy on one another, or businessmen who use these devices to spy on their competitors.

This form of mundane surveillance has also been featured in Arab drama. One Egyptian TV series, *Hatha al-Massa* (This Evening), for instance, broadcast in 2017, shed light on the practice of hacking mobiles; in one script, a mobile shop owner blackmails female clients in return for not disclosing their affairs which he discovered while hacking their mobile phones. Clients of that store were largely unaware of the hacking bugs installed by the shop owner. The series director, Tamer Mohsen, said in an interview that his concern was not only to alert people to the risk of hacking, 'I was not concerned with the cyber-hacking issue per se but I was interested in drawing people's attention to the dangerous idea that their smartphones can be lost, stolen, or hacked, exposing us to personal crises' (cited in Othman, 2017). There are other series that shed light on the same phenomenon including *Li-'ala Se'ir* (The Highest Bid) broadcast in 2017, which featured an ex-wife spying on her former husband's online accounts, while the series *Maloush Kabeer* (Unruly), broadcast in 2021, features a man spying on his wife. According to a BBC investigation (*BBC*, 2016), Internet blackmailing is a recurring problem in this region, where victims are threatened to be exposed with alleged video recordings of their illegal sexual relationships if they refuse to pay the demanded ransom. The BBC estimated that the number of such cases could be at least 1,000 in Jordan and more than 500 cases in the West Bank.

Mundane surveillance also includes non-state actors and individual hacking operations. For instance, the Kurdish movements and Islamist groups have engaged in hacking operations to express their views or their political opposition. The Iraq War in 2003 was one key instance of cyberwar and hacking operations between Iraqi insurgents and the US government (Al-Rawi, 2021, p. 11). Some Iraqi hackers also supported the public demonstrations in 2019 and attacked the Iraqi Ministry of Telecommunication website by posting a message referring to them as 'the people who refuse any foreign intervention in Iraq's internal affairs', in addition to hacking the social media accounts of the Iraqi Anti-Terrorism Squad Force (Al-Rawi, 2021, p. 109).

In Egypt, a Cyber Army was set up by Egyptian hackers who support the Egyptian military and see themselves as 'nationalist hackers' (Al-Rawi, 2021, p. 12). Groups such as the Muslim Brotherhood and its supporters, on the other hand, launched a series of hacking operations against Egyptian targets such as Cairo Airport and the Egyptian

28   *Infrastructure*

presidency websites (Al-Rawi, 2021, p. 110). A group called the Yemen Cyber Army ran several hacking operations against Saudi targets including the Saudi Ministry of Foreign Affairs. They submitted classified documents to *WikiLeaks* in 2015 (Al-Rawi, 2021, p. 78). Non-state actors and individual hackers resort to DIY hacking culture, learning from the numerous videos on *YouTube* as well as online hacking guides and fora (Al-Rawi, 2021, pp. 16, 107).

Surveillance has become a lifestyle and a culture in which all citizens may engage on a daily basis. It has thus been transformed 'from being an institutional aspect of modernity or a technologically enhanced mode of social discipline or control, it is now internalized and forms part of everyday reflections on how things are and of the repertoire of everyday practices' (Lyon, 2017, p. 825).

Conclusion

The Arab region is characterised as being the stage for proxy rivalries, not only among global powers but also among regional actors competing to influence the MENA environment. Examples abound of the use of media in the region as a tool in accentuating discord among Arab states, which further divided the region into sectarian, economic, and political loyalties (Mellor, 2018).

Moreover, it is expected that a new form of nationalism will become manifest in the digital sphere, where states are expected to be competing to invest and develop their own applications of machine learning and offensive and defensive cyber capabilities (Hogarth, 2018). The Arab states' investment in digital capabilities is not only predicated on funding but also on human developers, whose total number in the region is still small, although the majority of the population is young. This requires rigorous efforts to upskill young people to equip them for work in the cybersecurity industry (Booz Allen Hamilton, 2019, p. 3). A host of reasons compound the problem. Businesses do not always have the training and upskilling strategies, and vacancies for digital labour are usually filled by foreign labour pools. Graduates, moreover, tend to lack the skills required in the labour market, including digital skills, although the literacy rates have improved significantly across the region (Booz Allen Hamilton, 2019, pp. 8–11). Even graduates with cybersecurity degrees may need more upskilling to meet the demand of employers. This is why several rich states have launched digital training for their citizens, as will be discussed in Chapter 3.

Meanwhile, the GCC states compete to market themselves as the future digital hubs in the region. Bahrain for instance aspires to be a

Infrastructure   29

regional digital hub, especially after Amazon Web Services opened a data centre in Bahrain in 2019. Bahrain also seeks to collaborate with Chinese firms such as Huawei and China Telecom in addition to American Big Tech companies, although this has prompted the USA to warn Bahrain of the possible use of Chinese technology for espionage purposes. The economic downturn caused by the global pandemic, however, may force Bahrain and other GCC states, to seek cheap digital applications from China (Mogielnicki, 2020, p. 1). The UAE, moreover, is an example of a rich GCC state that exercises its soft power – not through ownership of media outlets across the region, but by hosting media-free zones for regional and international outlets in addition to hosting major media events such as the Arab Media Forum (Subeh, 2017). Saudi Arabia has also recently launched its new project, Media City in Riyadh, not only to compete with Dubai Media City but also to boost the image of the Saudi media sector. Leading networks such as the *MBC*, *al-Arabiya*, and *al-Hadath TV*, as well as the Saudi Research and Marketing group that owns the leading print press in the whole region, are to move to new premises in the new Media City by 2022/23 (Yaakoubi, 2021). The government aims to boost the image of the country abroad, with the help of innovative media technology and content created in several languages. There is some doubt, however, about the ability of this new Media City to compete with Dubai Media City which hosts more than 200 Arab and international outlets (*Al-Arab*, 2020 Feb. 6). There is also doubt concerning whether the Saudi media city will be limited to bringing back émigré outlets which are Saudi-owned but based outside the kingdom and whether Saudi Arabia can provide an attractive environment for leading international outlets to move to Riyadh.

Note

1 In fact, several global digital companies have offered applications that can track spouses and partners; for instance, a Japanese company offered an application that could track another person's whereabouts as well as their call log; in Australia, a company called Spouse Busters used similar measures to track partners through hidden voice recorders and secret microphones (Greff, 2013, 302–3).

References

Abrahams, Alexei & Andrew Leber (2021) Electronic Armies or Cyber Knights? The Sources of Pro-authoritarian Discourse on Middle East Twitter, *International Journal of Communication*, Vol. 15, pp. 1173–99.

30 *Infrastructure*

Abu Hamour, Mona (2018) Spying Between Spouses a Breach of Privacy. *al-Ghad* (in Arabic), April 6, 2018, https://bit.ly/3uC8csD

Akhbar al-Youm (2019, July 24) Fatwa About Spouse's Spying. (in Arabic), *Akhbar al-Youm*, https://bit.ly/3c5ho2n

Al-Arab (2020, Feb. 6) A Saudi Media City Under the Test of Restoring Émigré Platforms, *Al-Arab*, Vol. 42(11609), (in Arabic), p. 18.

Al-Arab (2020, Feb. 26) Egypt Closes Shiite Websites and Channels Causing Social Division, *Al-Arab*, Vol. 42(11629), (in Arabic), p. 18.

Al-Hattab, Khaled (2020) The "Electronic Army" Is Necessary for Kuwait. *Al-Qabas*, November 22, 2020, (in Arabic), https://bit.ly/3Hv2nEt

Al-Hurra (2021) *Electronic Armies in Iraq* (in Arabic), January 20, 2021, https://arbne.ws/330FycR

Al-Rawi, Ahmed (2021) *Cyberwars in the Middle East*. New Brunswick, NJ: Rutgers University Press.

Al-Saqaf, Walid (2016) Internet Censorship Circumvention Tools: Escaping the Control of the Syrian Regime, *Media and Communication*, Vol. 4(1), pp. 39–50, DOI: 10.17645/mac.v4i1.357

AUC/OECD (2021) *Africa's Development Dynamics 2021: Digital Transformation for Quality Jobs*. Paris: OECD, DOI: 10.1787/0a5c9314-en

BBC (2016, Oct. 26) Shame, Sex and Honour, www.bbc.com/arabic/features-37767119

Booz Allen Hamilton (2019) Engaging MENA Millennials in Cybersecurity Careers, https://www.boozallen.com/s/insight/publication/engaging-mena-millennials-in-cybersecurity-careers.html

Chang, Alexandra (2013) Why Undersea Internet Cables Are More Vulnerable Than You Think. *Wired*, April 2, 2013, https://www.wired.com/2013/04/how-vulnerable-are-undersea-internet-cables/

Coleman, Danielle (2019) Digital Colonialism: The 21st Century Scramble for Africa through the Extraction and Control of User Data and the Limitations of Data Protection Laws, *Michigan Journal of Race and Law*, Vol. 24, https://repository.law.umich.edu/mjrl/vol24/iss2/6

Crisp, Will & Suadad al-Salhy (2020) Inside Hezbollah's Fake News Training Camps. *The Telegraph*, August 2, 2020, https://www.telegraph.co.uk/news/2020/08/02/exclusive-inside-hezbollahs-fake-news-training-camps-sowing/

DiResta, Renée, Tara Kheradpir & Carly Miller (2020) "The World Is Swimming in a Sea of Rumors": Influence Operations Associated with El Fagr Newspaper (Egypt). *Stanford Internet Observatory*, April 2, 2020, https://fsi.stanford.edu/publication/april-2020-egypt-takedown

Dostor (2014, Nov. 24) Dostor Invades the Secret World of Spying Devices in Egypt (in Arabic), https://www.dostor.org/720810

Emara, Hussein (2018) NY Times Leaks about Jerusalem. *France24*, January 9, 2018, (in Arabic), https://bit.ly/3zyU4nP

ESCWA (2019). Digital Technologies for Development. Policy brief E/ESCWA/TDD/2017/3, https://www.unescwa.org/publications/arab-horizon-2030-digital-technologies-development

Infrastructure 31

FB (2020) Coordinated Inauthentic Behavior Report, October 2020, https://about.fb.com/news/2020/11/october-2020-cib-report/

Grossman, Shelby, Maria Fernanda Porras & Khadeja Ramali (2020) Hello from the Other Side: An Investigation into a Musical Pro-Muslim Brotherhood. Disinformation Operation. *Stanford Internet Observatory*, November 5, 2020, https://fsi.stanford.edu/publication/hello-other-side-investigation-musical-pro-muslim-brotherhood-disinformation-operation

Herbert, George & Lucas Loudon (2020) The Size and Growth Potential of the Digital Economy in ODA-Eligible Countries, K4D Helpdesk Report, December 1, 2020, Brighton: Institute of Development Studies.

Hoffman, Jon (2020) Espionage and Repression in the Middle East Courtesy of the West. *Open Democracy*, May 15, 2020, https://www.opendemocracy.net/en/north-africa-west-asia/espionage-and-repression-middle-east-courtesy-west/

Hogarth, Ian (2018) AI Nationalism, June 13, 2018, www.ianhogarth.com/blog/2018/6/13/ai-nationalism 1/24

Internet Society (2017) Enabling Digital Opportunities in the Middle East, October 2017, https://www.internetsociety.org/wp-content/uploads/2017/10/ISOC-Enabling-Digital-Opportunities-english-1.pdf

Ismail, Tareq (2021) Taxes on Digital Economy in the Arab States (in Arabic). *Arab Monetary Fund*, 2021, https://www.amf.org.ae/ar/study/taxes-digital-economy-arab-countries

Jamal, Ahmad (2021a) Transgressions of Egyptian Journalists Divides the Media Community, *Al-Arab*, Vol. 44(12161), August 27, 2021, (in Arabic), https://bit.ly/3utkJSA

Kirkpatrick, David (2018) Tapes Reveal Egyptian Leaders' Tacit Acceptance of Jerusalem Move. *NY Times*, January 6, 2018, http://www.nytimes.com/2018/01/06/world/middleeast/egypt-jerusalem-talk-shows.html

League of Arab States (2020) Arab Digital Economy Vision. Towards A Sustainable Inclusive and Secure Digital Future, January 2020, https://www.arab-digital-economy.org/09.pdf

Lotfi, Sumaya (2018) Big Data in the Arab States. *Arab Monetary Fund*, October 2018, (in Arabic), https://www.amf.org.ae/sites/default/files/research_and_publications/%5Bvocab%5D/%5Bterm%5D/%5Blanguage%5D/AMF%20Big%20data%20report_October%202%202018.pdf

Lyon, David (2017) Surveillance Culture: Engagement, Exposure, and Ethics in Digital Modernity, *International Journal of Communication*, Vol. 11, pp. 824–42.

Magnitt (2021, Mar. 11) ADQ Launches DisruptAD to Consolidate All Venture Capital Efforts, https://magnitt.com/news/adq-launches-disruptad-52545

Mainwaring, Sarah (2020) Always in Control? Sovereign States in Cyberspace, *European Journal of International Security*, Vol. 5, pp. 215–32.

Mellor, Noha (2018) The State of Arab Media Since 2011. *Mediterranean Yearbook 2018*. Barcelona: IeMED.

32 *Infrastructure*

Mogielnicki, Robert (2020) Sovereign Data: The Development and Marketing of Bahrain's Digital Domain. Issue Paper 11, December 30, 2020, Arab Gulf States Institute in Washington DC.

Mueller, Milton L. (2010) *Networks and States. The Global Politics of Internet Governance.* Cambridge, MA: The MIT Press.

Noman, Helmi (2019) Internet Censorship and the Intraregional Geopolitical Conflicts in the Middle East and North Africa, Research Publication No. 2019-1, January 2019, BERKMAN KLEIN CENTER FOR INTERNET & SOCIETY AT HARVARD UNIVERSITY, https://cyber.harvard.edu/story/2019-01/internet-censorship-and-intraregional-geopolitical-conflicts-middle-east-and-north

Othman, Alaa (2017) Hacking Mobiles and Users Look for Safety. *Al-Masry al-Youm,* August 10, 2017, (in Arabic), https://www.almasryalyoum.com/news/details/1175037

Pagliani, Paola (2020) Inclusive Citizenship and the Data Imperative in Arab Countries. Arab Human Development Report, NY: UNDP.

Privacy International (2016) New Investigation Reveals Syria's Mass Surveillance Ambitions and the Shadowy Western Surveillance Companies That Profit from It, December 12, 2016, https://privacyinternational.org/press-release/1311/new-investigation-reveals-syrias-mass-surveillance-ambitions-and-shadowy-western

Privacy International (2019a) State of Privacy Egypt, January 26, 2019, https://privacyinternational.org/state-privacy/1001/state-privacy-egypt

Privacy International (2019b) State of Privacy Morocco, January 26, 2019, https://privacyinternational.org/state-privacy/1007/state-privacy-morocco

PWC (2020) Global Media Outlook 2020–2024. Pulling the Future Forward: The Entertainment and Media Industry Reconfigures Amid Recovery. *PWC,* https://www.pwc.com/gx/en/industries/tmt/media/outlook.html

PWC (2021, April) Middle East Economy Watch. Rethinking the Role of Expats and Tax as We Look Beyond COVID-19, https://www.pwc.com/m1/en/publications/middle-east-economy-watch.html

Radcliffe, Damian & Handil Abuhmaid (2021) How the Middle East Used Social Media in 2020. *New Media Academy,* https://papers.ssrn.com/sol3/papers.cfm?abstract_id=3826011

Sasapost (2019, Sep. 22) *Twitter Suspended 4519 Accounts for a Network in UAE and Egypt* (in Arabic), https://sasapost.co/twitter-suspended-4519-accounts-for-a-network-in-uae-and-egypt/

Shires, James (2019) Hack-and-Leak Operations: Intrusion and Influence in the Gulf, *Journal of Cyber Policy,* Vol. 4(2), pp. 235–56, DOI: 10.1080/23738871.2019.1636108

Subeh, Ibrahim (2017) Understanding the Communication Strategies of the UAE, *Canadian Social Science,* Vol. 13(7), pp. 42–8, DOI:10.3968/9720

von Finckenstein, Valentina (2019) *Cybersecurity in the Middle East and North Africa,* July 2019. Beirut: Konrad Adenauer Foundation.

World Bank (2019) The Middle East and North Africa Human Capital Plan. Human Capital Project, https://thedocs.worldbank.org/en/doc/907071571420642349-0280022019/original/HCPMiddleEastPlanOct19.pdf

Yaakoubi, Aziz (2021) Saudi State Media Companies to Start Moving from Dubai to Riyadh, Reuters, September 4, 2021, https://www.reuters.com/world/middle-east/saudi-state-media-companies-start-moving-dubai-riyadh-2021-09-03

Zayani, Mohamed (2013) Al Jazeera's Palestine Papers: Middle East Media Politics in the post-WikiLeaks Era, *Media, War & Conflict*, Vol. 6(1), pp. 21–35.

2 Newsrooms

Introduction

The integration of technology inside newsrooms has developed through different stages, from processes such as cloning print content and sharing it online, to cross-promotion among various digital platforms. This chapter provides an overview of this integration process in Arab newsrooms. It shows how the online press, which emerged in the 1990s, aimed to provide an online or cloned copy of the print press. A period followed (during the 2000s) in which satellite television dominated the news and advertising market, although digital tools were still confined to the use of SMS and RSS for most television and print outlets. Post-2011, all news outlets realised the power of social media in reaching out to vast and young audiences, prompting these outlets to be innovative in creating, distributing, and sharing content across various platforms.

The following discussion does not present the development of every single Arab country, which is better explained in lengthier and more comprehensive handbooks (e.g., Miladi & Mellor, 2021) but seeks rather to highlight the development in major pan-Arab newsrooms. The overview below centres around the different stages of developing digital content, beginning with the cloned, online versions of newspapers, through to the rise of locally digital outlets post-2011. The chapter also touches on the massive decline of the Arab printed press, reflecting the dominance of satellite television in capturing the largest share of regional advertising revenue, coupled with the dominance of US Tech Giants such as *Google* in monopolising the digital advertising market in the region.

The beginning of the online press

It can be argued that Arab digital journalism has broadly progressed through three stages: the first stage, between 1995 and 1999, witnessed

DOI: 10.4324/9781003218838-3

Newsrooms 35

the launching of websites of major newspapers and the uploading of copies of the print editions onto those websites (Al-Raji, 2020). The pan-Arab (Saudi-owned) *Al-Sharq al-Awsat* newspaper published an electronic version of the print paper in 1995. This was followed by the Saudi-funded Lebanese newspaper *Al-Hayat* which published an electronic edition of the newspaper on CD-ROM and launched its electronic archive in the same year. Other newspapers in the region followed suit, such as the Kuwaiti *Al-Qabas*, publishing its content on CD-ROM in 1996, and the Lebanese newspapers *Al-Nahar* and *Al-Safir* (1997). Newspapers in Algeria began publishing online versions in 1997 with *El-Watan* (elwatan.com), followed by the French-language *Liberté* (liberte.com) and the Arabic newspapers *El-Youm* (elyoum.com) and *El-Khabar* (elkhabar.com) in 1998. The Moroccan online press was launched in the late 1990s with a few outlets creating e-copy of their newspapers or magazines such as *Maroc Hebdo* and *L'Economiste* (Benchenna & Marchetti, 2020). A few portals were also launched such as *Menara* in 1995 and *Wanadoo/Inwi* in 1999, curating content from newspaper websites, with or without the consent of the authors.

The second stage, from 2000 to 2010, marked the emergence of online news sites, independent of printed newspapers, and the rise of blogs written by professional journalists (Al-Raji, 2020, p. 29). There were several online newspapers which emerged during this period such as the Saudi *elaph.com* (2001) and the Lebanese *Al-Khabar* (2006). Many of these outlets were launched by professional journalists who found it easy to set up websites without much financial investment, lured by the promise of independent and unfettered journalism on the internet (Al-Raji, 2020, p. 31). In 2000, the online press in the Palestinian territories was said to begin during the *Al-Aqsa Intifada* in the same year, not only to advocate Palestinians' rights and to avoid Israeli censorship but also to communicate messages about the Palestinians' suffering to a global audience (Talahma 2012, pp. 47–9).

There were also several native online sites in Morocco such as *Yabiladi* and *Hespress*, accompanied by online advertising agencies such as *Pub Online* (Benchenna & Marchetti, 2020). Online news websites in Morocco initially provided duplicates of the information available offline. A 2010 survey of 18 Arabic- and French-language newspapers and magazines found that major television channels and radio stations in Morocco either updated the online content of those outlets from the print version or offered an archive service with some basic information (Zaid and Ibahrine, 2011, p. 23). By 2011, online

36 *Newsrooms*

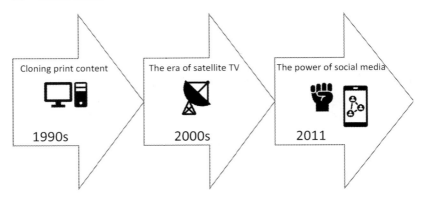

Figure 2.1 The development of online and digital media in the Arab region

news sites dominated the market, especially after the 2011 protests, and addressed the need to offer continuous news updates. Many of these news sites were created by former journalists who were not only critical of their media institutions but also of their role in the protest of February 2011 (*Hirak*), especially in state media (IJNET, 2021). By April 2018, Moroccan authorities had endorsed 892 media venture applications (Rammal, 2019, p. 44), of which one of the most prominent was *Hespress.com*, launched in 2007 as an independent online site that aggregated the news from other providers in the region. Other Moroccan ventures include *www.jawjab.ma*, *www.goud.ma*, *Al-YawmNas*, *Karayti.com*, *Le Desk*, *Conso news*, *Welovebuzz*, *Jawajab*, and *Smart media4you* (Rammal, 2019, p. 47). These online outlets, however, employed as few as 10 per cent of *recognised* journalists, defined as being members of the syndicates and holding press cards.

The third stage in the development of digital journalism has been ongoing since 2011, marked by the development of local digital outlets in the wake of the 2011 uprisings. This reflects the aspirations of citizens and journalists to create an alternative news format that would tap into the power of social media in reaching out to larger segments of the audience.

Post-2011 revolutionary media

The 2011 uprisings shed new light on Arab journalists' role as activists, with many journalists not seeing any contradiction between their political involvement and their professional objectivity. One editor at

Newsrooms 37

the privately-owned Egyptian newspaper *Al-Masry Al-Youm* defended this trend:

> We are no longer hiding our political agenda. We are becoming much more upfront and clearer about our political stance and our support for the revolution is becoming clearer in our editorial policy.
> (cited in Abdel-Sattar 2013, p. 216)

Al-Masry Al-Youm's site featured interactive maps inviting users to report election fraud cases during the 2011 parliamentary and the 2012 presidential elections (Abdel-Sattar 2013, p. 211). *Al-Masry Al-Youm* also encouraged print journalists to produce more videos as part of its efforts to converge multimedia production within the print newsroom (Abdel-Sattar, 2013, p. 338).

Following the 2011 uprising, Egyptian news outlets initially diverted their resources to social media to follow online activists – hailed as the engine of the uprising – and monitor the audience's debates. This trend began to fade, however, as the revolutionary euphoria started to wane. A survey of a sample of Egyptian journalists showed that following online activists was high on *Al-Ahram* newspaper's agenda (76 per cent in 2012, and 87 per cent in 2015), *Al-Masry Al-Youm* (77 per cent in 2012, and 71 per cent in 2015), and *Al-Watan* newspaper (90 per cent for the same period) reflecting the fast-paced political development during that phase: ousting President Mubarak in 2011, Political Islamists' winning the majority of seats in parliament in 2012, toppling President Morsi in 2013, and President al-Sisi's assumption of office in 2014. The motivation to follow online activists had declined by 2018, however. The percentage for *Al-Ahram* for example was 50 per cent, *Al-Masry Al-Youm* (60 per cent), and *Al-Watan* (52 per cent). Meanwhile, the interest in interacting with the audience, prioritised in 2012, witnessed a sharp decline in all outlets (El Gody, 2021, p. 63). Social media, nonetheless, are still used to identify content, depending on the news genre. A survey among Egyptian print journalists shows their frequent use of social media as a potential site for information and news stories, particularly about crime, business, technology, and religion, but less popular for finding political news (Mansour, 2018, p. 53). On the other hand, some editors in the state-newspaper *Al-Ahram* were sceptical of the impact of social media, seeing it as a 'trendy fad which would not last, and that *Al-Ahram*'s audience is traditionally-minded' (El Gody, 2021, p. 58). Still, the digital connection was regarded as part of the 'prestige of the organisation', more than as a tool for interacting with audiences (El Gody, 2021, p. 58).

38 *Newsrooms*

In Morocco, the number of online journalists increased from 98 in 2015 to 535 in 2018 (*Moroccan Ministry of Information*, 2018). The rise of the new cadre of online Arab journalists helped to introduce a new chapter for them in existing journalists' syndicates or even establish a new syndicate. This resulted in a new committee for Moroccan online journalists being set up in 2013, as part of the main Journalists' Syndicate. Efforts were made to create a code for online journalists who had been calling on the government to allow funding for online outlets similar to the print media (Zaid and Ibahrine, 2011, 72). A new syndicate was likewise formed for Jordanian online journalists in 2012. In Egypt, there used to be a polarisation of the profession between legacy media journalists and online journalists (Badr, 2020, p. 17). However, in 2020, after years of lobbying to be admitted into the Egyptian Journalists Syndicate, online journalists were finally accepted as members. This step was seen as an implicit admission of the increasing role of online news versus legacy media. Algeria, likewise, recognised the online press according to the media law of 2012.

The dilemma, however, is that online journalists have faced the problem of being subjected to multiple legal frameworks regulating online journalism, or what is described as 'legislative chaos', as the Head of the Journalists Syndicate in Jordan put it:

> It is wrong for a journalist or media organization to be prosecuted, sometimes by the penal code and at other times by the Publications and Publishing Law, the Cybercrime Law, the Communications Law, the Prevention Law on Terrorism, and State Security Law. This, of course, impedes freedoms, as the journalist cannot know their main legislative reference.
>
> (Al-Raji, 2020, pp. 162–3)

Lebanon likewise relied on criminal law, in the absence of rules governing online media, as a legal mechanism to penalise journalists, but that law is itself outdated and subject to much interpretation (*BBC Arabic*, 2021).

Inflated circulation figures

The emergence of online outlets has affected the printed press which has suffered a decline in readership. One report[1] claims that Arab newspapers still circulate millions of copies, but these figures are self-reported and inflated. Mansour (2018, p. 50), for instance, claims that the Egyptian *Al-Ahram* circulates 1 million copies per day, while the other two state-owned outlets – *Al-Akhbar* and *Al-Gomhuria* – distribute 800,000 and 750,000 copies, respectively. Other surveys estimate the Egyptian dailies' circulation figures to have declined from 2.4 million copies in 2009 to 400,000 copies in 2017 (Bazon, 2017). However, the former editor of *Al-Masry Al-Youm*, Hashim Qasim, claimed that many newspapers do not circulate more than 200 copies a day (Mamdouh, 2017). Qasim believes this reduced circulation of Egyptian newspapers is because they face challenges such as increasing printing costs, involving the high price of imported paper coupled with the declining value of the Egyptian Pound. Qasim also predicted the death of the printed press and recommended providing a subscription-based online news service to rescue the print media. He claimed that the advance in digital technology had forced many media institutions to offer their content for free, hoping to capture a share of the digital advertising revenue, but this proved difficult for many outlets (Mamdouh, 2017).

There are no reliable staff figures in Arab media, whether state or private outlets. The number of staff in Egyptian media institutions, particularly the state ones, for instance, is estimated to be around 21,000, of which 3,000–4,000 are journalists, with the remainder being administrative and technical staff.[2] Another survey estimated the number of journalists alone in the three leading Egyptian newspapers (*Al-Ahram*, *Al-Akhbar*, and *Al-Gomhuria*) to be around 3,520 (Mansour, 2018, p. 50), and another survey estimated the number of staff in all Egyptian media to be around 75,000 employees, including administrative staff (KFCRIS, 2018).

In Jordan, the number of news websites fell from 400 in 2011 to 175 in 2020 after the government imposed further amendments to the Press and Publications Law. This law redefined press publication to include online newspapers (Al-Raji, 2020, p. 32). The Jordanian government owns a large share of the daily *Al-Rai* newspaper (60 per cent) and *Ad-Dustor* (35 per cent); other print media such as *Al-Ghad* and *Al-Arab Al-Youm* newspapers have struggled financially due to the declining readership resulting in closure in 2014. *Al-Sabeel* closed its print version in 2019 and converted it to an online version (*USAID*, 2020, p. 3).

In Lebanon, there are around 500 news sites, operating with permission from the National Council for Audio-visual Media (*BBC Arabic*, 2021). In Algeria, the circulation of the print press declined by 80 per cent between 2010 and 2019 with the closure of 60 newspapers owing to the 60 per cent decline in advertising. This decline has also been exacerbated during the peak of COVID-19 (see Chapter 5). Online news in Algeria, on the other hand, was going through a state of chaos with

40 *Newsrooms*

the lack of regulations or vision for the digital sector in the country (Al-Arab, 2020, June 3).

As for the pan-Arab press market, it is mostly controlled by the Saudi Research & Media Group (SRG) with more than 30 pan-Arab titles including newspapers and magazines. SRG claims to have a monthly reach of 165 million readers (Serrano, 2021). *Al-Sharq al-Awsat* claims 235,000 copies, and *Arab News* 110,000 copies (*Arab News* is an English-language newspaper with a seemingly liberal editorial policy), while the pan-Arab *Al-Hayat* claims 166,000 copies. However, circulation figures, are unreliable as other sources claim that the circulation of *Arab News* is no more than 21,000. Pan-Arab newspapers also sell in limited numbers in individual Arab countries where local papers tend to be more popular, while most pan-Arab media subscriptions usually go to state institutions in the GCC states.

The SRG group recently announced its new rebranding plan to hone its digital provision, with the establishment of three new units: 'SRG Think' to conduct polling and provide media insight; 'SRG X' to lead events across the region, and 'SRG Labs' to lead on delivering training in content creation (Serrano, 2021).

Other Saudi online news sites operate with limited resources, such as *Elaph*, *Ajel News*, and *Sabq*, which depend heavily on content from international news agencies, and the reprinting of op-eds from leading Saudi dailies.

The quality generally varies among Arab digital outlets. An editor said that state outlets like the Egyptian *Al-Ahram* present rather 'boring content' despite their massive resources, and thus such state media have failed to re-brand themselves online (personal communication, 1 December 2021). Another journalist referred to the 'good examples' of outlets that have managed to integrate digital storytelling tools such as the Shorthand application. These are based in the GCC region such as the Saudi *Arab News*[3] and the Kuwaiti *Al-Qabas* (personal communication, 10 December 2021).

It is worth mentioning that both print and online markets face fierce competition from the numerous satellite television channels. The news market has witnessed an upsurge in the number of satellite channels since the end of the 1990s. They compete with both print and online news outlets and succeed in capturing a large share of the advertising market.

The power of satellite television

The 1991 Gulf War is regarded as the catalyst which triggered the so-called '*CNN* effect', referring to the dependence of Arab audiences on following the course of the war on *CNN* due to the lack of information on their state media. Following the war, the Arab media scene witnessed an explosion in the number of satellite channels, offering news and entertainment, moulded after American television shows. A decade later, the 9/11 attack on the USA marked a new watershed moment in the development of Arab media with the increasing interest of the US and European policymakers, as well as scholars, in Arab media output. *Al-Jazeera Arabic*, in particular, attracted much attention after it broadcast several tapes by Osama bin Laden. The Iraq War in 2003, was yet another catalyst that led to the establishment of several news satellite channels, chief among them is the Saudi-funded *Al-Arabiya*. Since then, hundreds of satellite channels have been established. The total number of such channels increased exponentially from 404 in 2006 to 1,300 in 2016, according to the Arab States Broadcasting Union (*asbu.net*). The most important pan-Arab news channels now are *Al-Jazeera Arabic*, *Al-Arabiya*, *Sky News Arabia*, and *Al-Mayadeen*. They compete with several Western-subsidised Arabic-language television such as *Alhurra* (USA), *BBC Arabic* (UK), *France 24 Arabic* (France), *DW Arabic* (Germany), and *CNN Arabic* (USA), in addition to *Russia Today/RT Arabic* (Russia) and the *CGTN Arabic* (China).

Saudi Arabia also controls the pan-Arab television market. The pan-Arab satellite carrier *Arabsat*, based in Saudi Arabia, can be used to exclude any channels deemed as a threat such as Iran's *Al-Alam TV*. The budgets of pan-Arab channels are never made public, but advertising is an important element. Major Saudi pan-Arab channels have been part of the *MBC* group since 1991 which includes *Al-Arabiya* (2003). The *MBC* group hosts channels dedicated to selected countries such as Egypt (*MBC Egypt*), Iraq (*MBC Iraq*), and *MBC5* (the Maghreb).

The political rivalry among GCC states has been extended to the media landscape with Qatar competing to establish its name as a new media hegemon in the region. Qatar's main channels are *Al-Jazeera* (1996) which has grown into a vast network encompassing *Al-Jazeera English* and a host of other specialist channels. The channel claims to have an audience of 220 million in 100 countries, but no reliable audience figures are available to verify this claim. *Al-Jazeera Arabic*, in fact, has seen a decline in its popularity since 2011, due to its support for the Muslim Brotherhood in Egypt and Syria, as well as its anti-Saudi stance. *Al-Jazeera Network* also founded *beIN Media Group* in 2014, with a portfolio of sports channels. *Fadaat Media Group* was also launched in Doha in 2012, and since 2014, it has produced *al-Araby al-Jadeed* newspaper and a website of the same name, and *Al-Araby TV (*2015) which broadcasts from London. Qatar's media empire also includes several digital ventures such as *AJ+* (an online channel run by *Al-Jazeera); Al-Quds Al-Araby* newspaper in London, and several pro-Muslim Brotherhood channels in Turkey, including *Mekameleen* and *Al-Sharq* (see Mellor, 2021). The news sites include *Sasapost, Noonpost,* and *Rasd*, in addition to *Al-KhaleejOnline* which is dedicated to content directed against UAE.

The web traffic and social media accounts of such satellite channels show a growing audience, but the data, collected by American companies, may not necessarily reflect genuine viewership or audience ratings if some institutions, for instance, buy clicks or followers. As of March 2021, the web traffic of the main pan-Arab TV channels shows *Al-Arabiya News* website has approximately 27 million visitors. Its main traffic comes from Saudi Arabia (42 per cent), Egypt (18 per cent), the USA (5 per cent), and UAE (4 per cent). This also reflects the main geographical focus of the channel's content, namely, news related to Saudi Arabia, Egypt, UAE, and the USA. The channel, launched in 2012, recently expanded its digital operations to create a virtual news studio, the first in the region (Townsend, 2019).

Sky News Arabia's website records 15 million visitors a month, of which the majority are from Saudi Arabia (37 per cent), followed by Egypt (29 per cent), the UAE (8 per cent), Kuwait (4 per cent), and Iraq (3 per cent). *Al-Jazeera* has recorded the highest traffic in the region, with more than 34 million visitors per month, but this includes visitors to *Al-Jazeera English*, who come primarily from the USA, India, and the UK.

Number of monthly web visitors in million

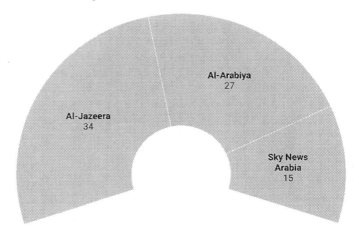

Figure 2.2 Web traffic for the three main pan-Arab news channels – compiled by the author from crunchbase.com, March 2021

The Saudi online news site *Sabq* on *Twitter* has the largest follower base of approximately 13 million, followed by *Al-Riyadh* newspaper and *Saudi 24 TV* (4.5 and 2.6 million, respectively). *Al-Arabiya* (with its two sites of which one is for breaking news) has a total of 34 million followers, while *Al-Jazeera* claims a following of approximately 16 million, and *Sky News Arabia* (two sites of which one is for breaking news) has 10 million.

Sky News Arabia on *Facebook* has the highest number of fans (16 million), while no other news channel features in the top 10 *Facebook* groups. The Saudi-owned *Rotana* channels (entertainment) have a follower base of 9 million, followed by *Arab News* and *Saudi Gazette* (5.4 and 2 million, respectively).[4]

The most accessed websites in Morocco include *Chouftv.ma*, *Almaghreb24.com*, and *Hespress.com*; while in Tunisia, the most popular local media websites are *Nessma.tv*, *Mosaiquefm.net*, and *Attessia.tv*. Algeria's most accessed outlets were *Ennahronline.com* and *Algerie360.com*, while in Egypt, *Youm7.com*, *Elwatannews.com*, *Dostor.org*, *Elmogaz.com*, and *Albawabhnews.com* are among the most popular news sites (figures from Alexa.com).

Finally, *Al-Jazeera Arabic* has over 8 million subscribers on *YouTube*, followed by *Al-Arabiya* with about 5 million subscribers, while local *Saudi TV* and *Al-Ikhbariyya* have nearly 1 million and 500,000 subscribers, respectively. *Sky News Arabia* has 1 million subscribers. Qatar's *Fadaat* (which owns *Al-Araby TV*) claims that its electronic platforms have more than 60 million views on social media platforms. Al-Araby TV has also launched a digital platform (*Ana Al-Araby*) dedicated to digital video content.[5]

These pan-Arab television channels are well-funded and able to afford an investment in the newest technology. *Al-Jazeera Network*, for instance, launched *Contrast VR* in 2017 – an immersive media studio – to produce 360-video and VR/AR content. The Executive Director of Digital at *Al-Jazeera*, Yaser Bishr said, 'The use of today's VR technologies is still in its infancy, but steadily growing in the Arab world and globally. With this in mind, *Al-Jazeera* produces unique stories, allowing viewers to live through real stories, immersed in fascinating experiences, excitement and hope' (cited in *Al-Jazeera*, 2017). The content, however, still comes with a basic level of interactivity such as moving between scenes. The problem with VR, AR, and 360-degree videos is the same one encountering pan-Arab media: not all audiences can afford a fast internet connection which allows them to benefit from such services, nor can they all afford the required headsets to enable them to watch this type of content.

44 *Newsrooms*

The advertising market has generally long been monopolised by the television sector, but now digital advertising revenue records the fastest growth in the region, forcing print, television, and online media to compete for the largest share. However, these sectors compete for only a fraction (estimated at 25–30 per cent) of the total digital advertising market, largely monopolised by the American Big Tech companies.

Losing the battle for digital advertising

While 2 per cent of newspapers' revenues came from digital advertising in 2008, this share reached about 17 per cent of the Arab advertising market by 2015 (Al-Raji, 2020, p. 46). There is no reliable data about the true volume of digital advertising in the MENA region, however. One estimate evaluated this market to be worth US$21 billion in the region, of which more than US$1 billion is generated in the Saudi market alone (Aoun, 2020). Another estimate assessed Arab digital advertising to be about US$6.2 billion in 2020 (Ismail, 2021, p. 8). An IPSOS report (17 May 2021) estimated the total advertising (online and offline) to be worth circa US$3.1 billion in 2020 (dropping from US$4 billion in 2019), of which the digital advertising spend was estimated to be US$ 1.29 billion in 2020. Another report (IAB, 2021) estimated the total MENA digital advertising market to be around US$3,6 billion in 2020 – which is only 14 per cent of the advertising spend in a country such as the UK (US$25,7 billion) for the same year. It is, however, safe to assume that the online advertising market is growing, as poll after poll documents the increasing congregation online, especially among young people.

According to one estimate by IPSOS, about 70 per cent of online advertising revenue in the region goes to the Tech Giants *Facebook* and *Google* (Ahmad, 2020). The market for digital advertising in Morocco, for instance, is largely monopolised by *Google* and *Facebook*, which control 70 per cent of advertising revenue (Laktawi, 2021). A large number of Moroccan news websites depend on modest private funding apart from a handful of sites which are part of advertising agencies. Outlets usually offer free content, except *ledesk.ma* which is a subscription-based site launched in 2015. Its founder claimed to have raised more than euro 700,000 but failed to secure the target of 10,000 subscribers in the first year of operation. This forced the site to operate under a combination of the paywall and freemium models (Benchenna & Marchetti, 2020). To sustain their operations, some Moroccan online ventures such as *9rayti.com* obtain part of their revenue from selling users' data, while other ventures such as *Smart media4you* depend on monthly or annual subscriptions (Rammal, 2019,

p. 84). In any case, the problem with sustaining such online ventures is that the lion's share of revenue goes to *Google* and *Facebook* and not to local outlets (Benchenna & Marchetti, 2020).

The print press in Tunisia has been struggling to cope with its declining readership and advertising revenue since 2010; consequently, the number of outlets decreased from 255 to only 50 in 2018. One such newspaper, *Al-Sareeh*, announced in April 2018 that it had to shut down because of the rising cost of materials such as paper, ink, and printing plates, coupled with the deterioration of the price of the local currency (Moammari, 2018). The daily circulation of Tunisian newspapers did not exceed 100,000 copies, and its advertising revenue did not exceed US$6.7 million, which is a fraction of the total advertising spend in Tunisia – approximately US$100 million.

It is claimed that the Arab printed press had a media market share of 45 per cent in 2010, declining to 32 per cent in 2015, especially in Egypt and the UAE, where 50 per cent of the newspaper organisations were shut down during that period, while many digital news sites were being established (KFCRIS, 2018). The Saudi media share is by far the largest, given that the Saudi economy is also the largest in the region at about 21 per cent of MENA's total GPD, even though Saudi Arabia's population constitutes only 5.7 per cent of the region's total (IPSOS, March 8, 2021). It is, therefore, unsurprising that many Arab media outlets across the region used to compromise their content if deemed inappropriate for the Saudi consumer (Farzat, 2017). Saudi newspapers used to receive a large share of the advertising market, amounting to millions of US dollars per outlet per year. Managers of those newsrooms, however, did not know how to re-invest the profits; instead, they wasted the money on futile projects, according to the former editor Abdel Wahab al-Fayez (cited in Al-Daghfaq, 2017). The deputy editor of *Okaz* newspaper also said that the profits of *Okaz* used to reach more than US$133 million per year, but most of this money went to building new offices instead of planning for the fierce digital competition. However, many editors believed that the main competitors were digital newspapers, and therefore they invested in setting up new websites for their outlets while overlooking the fact that the main competitors were the American Tech Giants who controlled social media sites. The result was that many newspapers lost more than 70 per cent of their advertising revenue; only the newspapers with strong cash flows such as *Al-Riyadh* newspaper could survive the current market. The problem, according to Saudi editors, was also because of the need to diversify their income sources so that the print press would not have to depend solely on advertising contracts (Al-Daghfaq, 2017).

46 *Newsrooms*

The news institutions' share of digital advertising in Kuwait was likewise in decline, although the budgets dedicated to digital political campaigns – usually during parliamentary elections – were estimated to be between US$165 and US$330 million. However, the funds raised during these campaigns are being run on individual candidates' *YouTube* channels or *Instagram* accounts, instead of being used to purchase advertising spaces in newspapers or local digital news sites (Farzat, 2017).

In Yemen, social media sites such as *Facebook* have been the go-to source for updates on the development of the situation in the country, since the 2011 uprising. The transfer of power to President Abd Rabbo Mansour Hadi of Yemen meant his son assumed the task of managing online propaganda in favour of his father's government while attacking his opponents. He has therefore created scores of news sites, not only to attract Yemeni audiences but also to dominate the search engines used by Yemenis. By the end of 2017, there were 258 outlets in Yemen: some were affiliated with the government and others with the Houthis (Mellor, 2021). This encouraged various news sites to subscribe to *Google Ads* as the most important revenue source, forcing those sites to compete among themselves to attract as many audiences as possible, to enable them to double their advertising revenue, even at the expense of providing serious and meaningful content (Khashafa, 2021). *Google* typically shares the profits with the publisher, but the profits depend on the number of clicks *Google* Ads receives. This means that if the reader does not click on any advertisement, there will be no financial return for the publisher. The dependence of these news sites on *Google Ads* pushed those sites to use sensational headlines to attract readers and increase the traffic on their sites. One Yemeni editor, Amer Al-Dumaini, argued that *Google Ads* not only contributed to the deterioration of the Yemeni online press but also to the weakening of its content; this eventually led to declining confidence in the Yemeni journalistic content. Al-Doumaini explained:

> *Google*'s aim is purely commercial, and online journalistic sites have had to promote sensational content to draw attention to get the greatest number of visits, thus maximizing profits. The profession has turned into a means of livelihood and earning, instead of providing serious and professional content; consequently, many people from outside the journalism field have joined the profession in search of profit. We have witnessed the rise of dozens of news websites whose number has continuously multiplied, while the serious online press has remained in the hands of a few outlets.
>
> (cited in Khashafa, 2021)

Another Yemeni web developer confirmed this trend (cited in Khashafa, 2021):

> There is a wave of news sites that pursue sensationalism in their headlines, and profit from *Google Ads* to the detriment of accuracy. Readers find sensationalist headlines and click on the links to the relevant news stories only to get fragmentary information.

The advantage for *Google* is to create more traffic on those sites for its advertisers, with the price per click ranging between US$0.01 and US$0.15 or even more, depending on the location of both advertisers and readers. One editor said that digital advertising spending is uneven across the region, so an advertiser may spend one dollar in Saudi Arabia but only five cents in Egypt (personal communication, 1 December 2021). It is not clear how much a Big Tech such as *Facebook* shares with publishers across the Arab region, but one estimate was US$10 to US$20 million annually, but there are no reliable figures to verify such individual estimates. If the estimate was correct, this would be a fraction of *Facebook*'s digital ad revenue in the region (estimated between only US$800 million and US$ 1 billion in 2020), and a small market compared to *Facebook*'s total advertising revenue, US$84 billion in the same year (Solon, 2021). Also, digital advertising revenue, even in the wealthy GCC region, is not comparable to that in the USA, where advertisers spend relatively more, because most advertising revenues come from North America; and *Facebook* declared in its annual report in 2020 that approximately 47 per cent of its advertising revenue comes from the USA and Canada.

The distribution of market shares begs the question as to why Arab digital content has increased post-2011. One key motivation to set up such outlets was the political optimism in the wake of the 2011 uprisings. Journalists and editors hoped they could establish alternative media; however, these journalists, including those who had managed to obtain funding from Western media donors, discovered that local digital outlets were not sustainable without advertising revenue or subscription fees. Arab audiences have, so far, declined to pay for the news, but accept paying for digital entertainment applications such as *Shahid* and *Netflix*. Another reason is that many journalists see a source of quick income and profit in local digital outlets and many websites have been launched in the hope of being able to sell them to the highest bidder in the GCC states. One editor told me that the Internet is jammed with news sites of all genres, with each wanting to make a quick profit but many sites are staffed by amateurs. He said that if

48 *Newsrooms*

he gets a proposal to acquire such a site in a populous state like Egypt with a huge follower base, he may not see it as a good asset, compared to a site in the richer GCC region (personal communication, 1 December 2021).

In summary, American Tech Giants such as *Google*, *Facebook*, *Apple*, and *Microsoft* have defined the region's digital technology. *Google*, *YouTube*, *Facebook*, and *Twitter* have topped the most accessed websites in the region. The decline of Arab print media is not only due to the competition of digital platforms, but also the result of retaining a traditional business model which depends on owners' injecting money into the outlet, generous advertising contracts, and readers' subscriptions. One difficulty facing online outlets in attracting advertisers is the monopoly of the American Tech Giants who seize the lion's share of the market; another difficulty is the shortage of digitally-skilled staff who can keep pace with the accelerating technology (Al-Raji, 2020, p. 100). One journalist who set up his own blog told me that the main issue is the lack of digital training (personal communication, 28 August 2021). This has prompted many well-funded pan-Arab outlets to launch their own digital training initiatives to address this problem, as will be discussed in the following chapter.

Conclusion

In early 2021, the Australian government introduced its new legislation to force Tech Giants such as *Google* and *Facebook* to pay local news media for the news feed circulated on their platforms. Consequently, *Google* rushed to strike deals with two major media companies in Australia to pay for their shared news (Cave, 2021). An Iraqi commentator described Mark Zuckerberg as the 'Supreme Leader of *Facebook*', alluding to his massive power in the global digital media sector, and wrote that the Australian controversy raised many questions about the acceptable business models for news outlets while urging Arab media to define what they wanted from the Tech Giants, rather than the other way round (Nei'ma, 2021). The Australian case prompted many governments to ponder on a similar action to force the American Big Tech corporations to pay for local journalism; however, a similar action is unlikely to occur in the Arab region, as many states fear facing reduced services by the Big Tech giants such as *Facebook*.

Indeed, Arab media seem to surrender to the dominance of American Tech Giants which have doubled their profits while revenue from the Arab news market has declined. This has led to the axing of many newsrooms, especially those which have built their economic model on advertising revenue. These Tech Giants have transformed themselves into 'a new dictator model which has the main say in editorial decisions, the definition of news content, and directing users' behaviour (Al-Sahafa, 2021, p. 3). One possible solution is for governments to purchase advertising to support local newsrooms (Schiffrin, Clifford & Tumiatti, 2021, p. 25); however, if such a solution was implemented in the Arab region, it may be interpreted as yet another attempt by the state to intervene in the media sphere, and thus control public opinion.

The declining print press combined with the shrinking share of the digital advertising market has led to partial dependence on Western media donors to fund new digital initiatives. Several ventures include digital media start-ups which have received donations from Western organisations such as *Mada Masr* in Egypt, and *Inkyfada* in Tunisia (*USAID*, 2020, p. 4). Other outlets subsidised by foreign donors include *Madaba Hawana* in Jordan, which is a community radio supported by the EU and broadcasting through *Facebook* (*USAID*, 2020, p. 4). It is difficult, nonetheless, for such ventures to sustain the funding stream, especially as Arab users generally prefer not to pay for news. The founder of *Fatabayyanu*, Moath Althahe, for instance, said that the problem of financial instability limits digital start-ups to expand their operations, and existing funding may not even cover the team's wages; this means such start-ups may partially depend on volunteers (Rammal, 2019, p. 105). The next chapter sheds some light on those editors and journalists who see themselves as media entrepreneurs.

References

Abdel-Sattar, Nesrine (2013) "Innovation in Arabic Online Newsrooms: A Comparative Study of the Social Shaping of Multimedia Adoption in Aljazeera Net, Almassae and Almasry Alyoum in the Context of the Arab Spring." Unpublished PhD diss., Oxford Internet Institute, University of Oxford.

Ahmad, Yasser (2020) The Stats of Digital Advertising in MENA Region, September 20, 2020, https://consultyasser.com/stats-digital-advertising-in-the-mena/

Al-Arab (2020, June 3) Algeria Encourages Digital Transformation of the Press, *Al-Arab*, Vol. 43(11720), (in Arabic), p 18, https://bit.ly/2SM8FeW

Al-Daghfaq, Hoda (2017) Saudi Press: Need to a Different Investment Model. *al-Faisal*, June 30, 2017, (in Arabic), https://www.alfaisalmag.com/?p=5482

Al-Jazeera (2017, Apr. 12) Al-Jazeera Launches Contrast VR Platform, https://bit.ly/3NJBDmD

50 Newsrooms

Al-Raji, Mohamad (ed.) (2020) *The Environment of Arab Online Press-Contexts and Challenges* (in Arabic). Doha: Al-Jazeera Centre for Studies.

Al-Sahafa (2021) editorial, *Al-Sahafa* magazine (in Arabic), Vol. 6(21), Spring 2021, Doha: Al Jazeera Media Institute, p. 3.

Aoun, Elie (2020) MENA Advertising Expenditure Dissected, IPSOS, May 12, 2020, https://www.ipsos.com/en-ae/mena-advertising-expenditure-dissected

Badr, Hanan (2020) The Egyptian Syndicate and (Digital) Journalism's Unresolved Boundary Struggle, *Digital Journalism*, DOI: 10.1080/21670811.2020.1799424

Bazon, Ahmad (2017) The Crisis of Lebanese Press. *Al-Faisal Magazine*, June 30, 2017, (in Arabic), https://www.alfaisalmag.com/?p=5448

BBC Arabic (2021, May 3) International Press Day: Will Digital Journalism Bring in More Freedoms? https://www.bbc.com/arabic/middleeast-56966719

Benchenna, Abdelfettah & Dominique Marchetti (2020) Writing Between the 'Red Lines': Morocco's Digital Media Landscape. *Media, Culture & Society*, DOI: 10.1177/0163443720972316

Cave, Damien (2021) Google Is Suddenly Paying for News in Australia. What About Everywhere Else? *The New York Times*, February 17, 2021.

El Gody, Ahmed (2021) Convergence and Divergence of ICTs in Egyptian Newsrooms: A Longitudinal Approach, *Journal of African Media Studies*, Vol. 13(1), pp. 53–71, DOI: 10.1386/jams_00033_1

Farzat, Adnan (2017) The Gulf Press Laments Advertising Revenues and Searches for Alternatives. *Al-Faisal Magazine*, June 30, 2017, (in Arabic), https://www.alfaisalmag.com/?p=5473

IAB (2021, September 22) MENA Adspend in 2020. Dubai: The Interactive Advertising Bureau (IAB), https://iabgcc.com/wp-content/uploads/2021/07/MENADigitalAdspend2020-Report_vf.pdf

IJNET (2021, Feb. 27) Digital Journalism in Morocco, https://ijnet.org/en/node/9726

IPSOS (2021, May 17) The Anatomy of MENA 2020 Ad Spend, https://www.ipsos.com/en-eg/anatomy-mena-2020-ad-spend

IPSOS (2021, Mar. 8) Saudi Arabia 2021. Attractiveness and Uncertainties. 10 Key Points, https://www.ipsos.com/en-sa/flair-saudi-arabia-2021-attractiveness-and-uncertainties

Ismail, Tareq (2021) Taxes on Digital Economy in the Arab States (in Arabic). Arab Monetary Fund, 2021, https://www.amf.org.ae/ar/study/taxes-digital-economy-arab-countries

KFCRIS (2018) Future of Print Press in the Arab World, October 22, 2018, King Faisal for Research and Islamic Studies, (in Arabic), https://kfcris.com/ar/eve/view/132

Khashafa, Amjad (2021) How Google Ads Ruined Digital Journalism in Yemen (in Arabic). *Al-Mashad*, March 10, 2021, https://www.almashhad-alyemeni.com/197104

Laktawi, Majida Ait (2021) Moroccan Press Is Dying Slowly (in Arabic). *al-Quds al-Arabi*, March 16, 2021.

Mamdouh, Wael (2017) Interview with Hisham Wasim. *al-Masry al-Youm*, June 13, 2017, (in Arabic), https://www.almasryalyoum.com/news/details/1148299

Mansour, Essam (2018) The Adoption and Use of Social Media as a Source of Information by Egyptian Government Journalists, *Journal of Librarianship and Information Science*, Vol. 50(1), pp. 48–67.

Mellor, Noha (2021a) Media in Yemen – Narratives of Polarization and Fragmentation, in Miladi and Mellor (eds.) *Routledge Handbook of Arab Media*. London: Routledge, pp. 491–501.

Miladi, Noureddine & Noha Mellor (2021) *Routledge Handbook on Arab Media*. London: Routledge.

Moammari, Mohamad (2018) The Crisis of the Paper Press in Tunisia (in Arabic), *al-Araby al-Jadeed*, April 4 2018, https://bit.ly/3jgnZeL

Moroccan Ministry of Information (2018) Indicators of Free Press, 2018, (in Arabic), http://www.mincom.gov.ma/a/wp-content/uploads/sites/2/2019/05/Indicateurs-liberte-presse.pdf

Nei'ma, Karam (2021) Once again with the Supreme Leader of Facebook (in Arabic), *Al Arab*, Vol. 43(119) 84, (in Arabic), February 27, 2021, p. 18.

Rammal, Ali (2019) Digital Media Startup Companies in the Arab World. The Examples of Lebanon, Morocco and Jordan. Maharat Foundation. http://maharatfoundation.org/media/1810/digital-media-startup-companies-in-the-arab-world-2019.pdf

Schiffrin, Anya, Hannah Clifford & Kylie Tumiatti (2021) *Saving Journalism: A Vision for the Post-Covid World*. Washington DC: Konrad-Adenauer-Stiftung.

Serrano, Sofia (2021) Saudi Research & Media Group Announces Transformation Strategy. *Campaign Middle East*, July 11, 2021, https://campaignme.com/saudi-research-media-group-announces-transformation-strategy-focusing-on-platform-expansion-and-international-part%E2%80%A6

Solon, Olivia (2021) Facebook battles reputation crisis in the Middle East. NBC News, May 29, 2021, https://www.nbcnews.com/tech/social-media/facebook-battles-reputation-crisis-middle-east-n1269026

Talahma, Thair Mohamed (2012) "Gatekeeping and Interactive Media on the Palestinian News Sites on the Internet" (in Arabic). Unpublished Master's thesis, Middle East University, Jordan.

Townsend, Sarah (2019) Sky News Arabia to Expand with Virtual Reality, Digital and Content Upgrades. *The National*, April 28, 2019, https://www.thenationalnews.com/business/markets/sky-news-arabia-to-expand-with-virtual-reality-digital-and-content-upgrades-1.854299

USAID (2020) Jordan Media Assessment, June 9, 2020, https://pdf.usaid.gov/pdf_docs/PA00WQVH.pdf

Zaid, Bouziane & Mohamed Ibahrine (2011) *Mapping Digital Media: Morocco*. London: Open Society Media Program.

Notes

1 Mideastmedia, http://www.mideastmedia.org/industry/2016/newspapers/#s32
2 BBC Arabic (6 October 2020), Betwaqeet Misr, https://www.youtube.com/watch?v=uswA-ZSpqbw
3 One example is this news story about Arabic calligraphy: https://www.arabnews.com/ArabicCalligraphy
4 Figures from Semrush.com and crunchbase.com, collected in March 2021.
5 See https://www.alaraby.com/video-categories/video-category-50

3 Journalists

Introduction

Arab journalists have been seen as partners in the region's developmental plans in the post-independence Arab states, but this role has declined, leaving journalists feeling that they are merely ordinary salaried employees (As-Shawabka, 2021, p. 70). The first half of this chapter provides a discussion of the changing attributes of Arab journalists, ranging from seeing them as partners in nation-building to using them as propaganda tools in regional and international conflicts. In fact, some Arab officials admit to the difficulty of remaining neutral in reporting about conflicts involving their states while several journalists expressed similar views in favour of a more nationalist narrative, which is often hostile to other states (Alhussein, 2019). Arab digital media has also challenged the traditional definition of a journalist as one who is remunerated for gathering and editing news reports, with the rise of citizen journalists who gather, curate, and edit online content. The second half of this chapter, therefore, sheds new light on the attributes of modern journalists as entrepreneurs and technologists.

Journalists as partners in nation-building

The second half of the 20th century witnessed the political independence of many Arab states who sought to mobilise their populations with the aim of national development. The then-nascent Arab media scholarship reflected this trend, with many scholars preferring to describe Arab media systems in terms of either social responsibility or development theory, by acknowledging that media should serve for the development and political stability needed for these societies (Mellor, 2005, p. 50). Many scholars in the Global South resorted to the concept of the social responsibility of journalism – introduced by

DOI: 10.4324/9781003218838-4

54 *Journalists*

the American Commission on Freedom of the Press in the 1950s – as an ideal press system – in theory. The developmental journalism in the region then aimed at supporting national developmental plans (see, e.g., Al-Hefnawy, 2014), usually focusing on topics such as citizenship, national identity, the effect of Western culture on Arab youth, the hegemony of Western values and culture, and the future of the Arabic language (see, e.g., Al-Abdallah, Qotb & Turban, 2017). The concept fell out of favour since the 1990s, however, with the efforts to demote governments' interventions in the media sphere. Arab journalists realised then that traditional news values (focusing on the elites) were not suited to their national needs especially in the wake of the 1991 Gulf War and the explosion of the number of satellite television channels since then, as discussed in the previous chapter. During the 1990s, and at the peak of the globalisation debate, Arab media scholars and journalists also warned against the increasing dependency on international (American) news providers and the penetration of American values into Arab societies (Mellor, 2007). This is why many newsrooms, especially television satellite channels like Al-Jazeera or Al-Arabiya, expanded their network of correspondents to reflect their independence as newsmakers.

In the wake of the 2011 uprisings, the debate about journalists' role centred on 'constructive journalism', defined as the practice of highlighting positive angles in the news stories as well as positive stories about one's country. While some Arab journalists see this form of journalism as a tool for nation-building, others see it as a risk in attributing such positiveness to state propaganda. One Egyptian journalist in *Al-Masry al-Youm* newspaper feared that such 'positive' news may be interpreted as propaganda:

> Positiveness has a bad reputation in the Arab mindset. It is usually attributed to the concept of propaganda or appraisals to regime officials. National media in the Arab countries have a long history of highlighting officials' activities and personnel rather than focusing on the news itself and its impact on the audience. This excessive usage of positive news and exaggeration led to audiences' loss of credibility in the national media.
>
> (Cited in Allam, 2019, p. 1287)

This is particularly the case in Arab news outlets, as many news institutions tend to depend on official sources. In Lebanon, for example, traditional media tend to rely almost entirely on governmental and political elites as news sources, and the same sources have dominated *tweets* discussing the news (Kozman & Cozma, 2021). The same trend is noticed in other countries where journalists draw on politicians and experts as their main sources.

Moreover, some Arab journalists have established their own PR practices to aid politicians and businessmen in (re-)branding themselves, benefiting from the expanding PR market. For instance, Egyptian politicians now recruit such PR companies to act as their spokespersons (Fikry, 2019, p. 18). A number of those PR companies are owned by journalists and television enterprises that work with foreign embassies or corporations in Egypt. If a public project or initiative faces criticism, a PR company can immediately record a video with ordinary citizens as 'vox pops' to talk about the project positively, then post that video on social media sites. PR companies also manage the social media sites of public figures; many journalists are also enticed with gifts to write favourable stories about certain personalities or ministers.

Many other journalists, meanwhile, are victimised and entrapped in national and regional conflicts in countries such as Egypt, Syria, Libya, Lebanon, Sudan, and Morocco. In the following, I provide some examples of harassment to journalists via surveillance and/or prosecution.

Trapped in proxy wars

The Egyptian state's control of the media sphere has been evident since 2014, and its crackdown on journalists is usually attributed to publishing 'fake news'. In 2016, for example, two Egyptian online journalists were charged with publishing false news when they were not even recognised as members under the rules of the Journalists' Syndicate since online journalists were not given press cards at that time (Badr, 2020, p. 9). Surveillance of journalists is also claimed to be a common practice in Egypt. The former editor of the private newspaper *Al-Masry al-Youm*, Hashim Qasim, claimed that staff access to the 28th floor of the state television building, *Maspero*, was prohibited because it had sophisticated cameras installed showing everything happening in Tahrir Square, where the 2011 uprisings began (*Arabi21*, 2019). Qasim also claimed that the building was staffed by 6,000 security guards – a figure that was disputed by a state official who said that the real number was 3,000 (*Arabi21*, 2019). The state, moreover, allegedly acquired private outlets such as *Al-Masry al-Youm* newspapers, which used to be owned by the businessman Salah Diab, and *Al-Mehwar TV*, which used to be owned by Hasan Ratib. This meant that all media institutions would be expected to endorse state policies (Hafez, 2021).

56 *Journalists*

Despite the state's omnipotent power, Egyptian journalists displayed some autonomy when they felt threatened by state officials. For instance, several journalists, editors, and TV presenters in state outlets mobilised to call for the resignation of the former Minister of Information, Osama Heikal, after he declared that Egyptian media content was unattractive to the young people who flocked to digital and international media instead (Omar, 2020). That statement agitated many journalists to launch a campaign against the minister, accusing him of 'treason'; many state-owned media, including national television, dedicated airtime and newspaper space to attacking the minister. The criticism marks an unprecedented and unexpected move by journalists in a country where media is almost totally controlled by the government. The tension shed light on the lack of reliable audience data, with state statistics claiming newspaper circulation as millions of copies each year, and editors of privately owned newspapers claiming that the real figures did not exceed thousands of copies for all state and private newspapers combined (Meghawer, 2018). A similar forceful reaction by journalists and the Supreme Council of Media was recorded in 2021, after a media professor posted a comment on *Facebook*, accusing Egyptian talk show presenters of lacking professionalism, resulting in a wave of complaints against the professor (*Al-Sharq al-Awsat*, 2021). It is worth noting that journalists' aggressive reaction, in these two examples, was mostly justified by their fear of losing their job if the debate about audience rating continued. When it comes to political debates, however, journalists usually resort to self-censorship to avoid problems with the state and to maintain their positions in their organisations.

Journalists in other countries also faced massive legal and professional constraints. In Sudan, for instance, the government banned two Sudanese newspapers (*al-Rai* and *Sudani*) and two television stations (*al-Shorouk* and *al-Andalus*) on charges that they received funding from the regime of former President Omar Al-Bashir, who was overthrown in April 2019. The Sudanese state-owned television channels are under the control of the government, while private stations are claimed to be owned by powerful businessmen with links to the Political Islamist movement, Muslim Brotherhood. In Morocco, online journalists can be targeted with spyware such as the Journalist Omar Radi, who was working on the *Hirak* protest movement in 2017 when he became a victim of spyware. He was later arrested on allegations of rape (Benchenna & Marchetti, 2020). In the Palestinian territories, groups of hackers affiliated with the Palestinian security service which used spyware to target journalists and activists were closed down by

Facebook (IFEX, 2021). In Lebanon, factionalism and institutional-ised sectarianism which have been prevailing since the 1975 civil war, have extended to the media field with each faction establishing its own media outlets to defend its ideology (Kozman & Cozma, 2021, p. 1002), not to mention regional pressures on news institutions. The Lebanese press, for instance, lost much of its advertising revenues from the GCC states as a consequence of the recent political conflict. Gulf newspapers have not only attracted more advertising revenue but have also managed to lure Lebanese and Arab journalists with higher wages and better benefits compared to their native countries (Bazon, 2017).

In Syria, the civil war has marked one of the most extensive cyber-wars in the region between both the regime and the Syrian Electronic Army, on the one hand, and rebels led by the Syrian Free Army (and their Western and regional supporters) on the other. Both sides have engaged in using digital media to disseminate disinformation and propaganda (Shehabat, 2013). The country ended up being the site for a proxy war between two sides: the USA, France, and the UK in alliance with Turkey, Saudi Arabia, Israel, and Qatar, on one hand, and Syria, Russia, and Iran on the other (Robinson, 2019). When the uprisings began in 2011, the regime shut down the mobile network and internet connections in some cities such as Homs and Darra. Proxy modems and satellite phones were used by rebels and powered by Jordanian and Turkish SIM cards and Saudi satellite phones, to document the clashes with the regime and send reports to international broadcasters such as *Al-Jazeera* (Shehabat, 2013). The Syrian Free Army soon set up its *Facebook* page and press centre to disseminate its news and keep a record of the killings, while the Syrian Electronic Army set up cloned *YouTube* pages to trap and track activists inside Syria. In return, some Syrian activists hacked the Syrian president's private email address, and the leaked emails were published in the *Guardian* and reported on *al-Arabiya* channel (Shehabat, 2013).

There were also numerous Western-funded media outlets which attracted many activists and trained them in reporting news from the field, although it was difficult to define these activists as professional journalists (*The Syrian Centre for Media and Freedom of Expression*, 2021, p. 6). However, news from Syria was often difficult to verify, with each party using new and legacy media to exaggerate the doings of the other. For instance, the use of toxic chemicals incident in Douma, Syria, in April 2018 was the centre of much speculation. The Office for the Prevention of Chemical Weapons (OPCW) confirmed the incident, although leaked documents published by *Wikileaks* cast doubt on the event being conducted by the Syrian regime, and the extent

58 *Journalists*

of casualties (wikileaks.org/opcw-douma/). American (and European) media meanwhile, represented the situation in Syria in a way that justified more Western military intervention, while referring to terrorist groups such as Jabhat al-Nusra[1] in East Aleppo as 'the opposition', thereby concealing the fact that not all residents wanted to remain in areas held by the rebels or al-Nusra (Cockburn, 2017, p. 2). Moreover, no consideration was given to the extent and consequences of such an intervention, despite the massive human and financial losses incurred from previous ones such as in Libya or Iraq (Shupak, 2018).

In Libya, the media sector still bears the brunt of the ongoing conflict and chaos that has swept the country since 2011. One of the main issues has been the division and conflict coupled with the fragmentation of media institutions, and the divisive media discourse, whether in public or private media. The majority of private outlets operate from outside Libya, mostly in other MENA countries, save for a few channels still operating from Tripoli or Benghazi. Journalists have become easy targets for militias and other groups. Eighty-three journalists were subject to attacks or assaults between 2018 and 2019 alone, and this figure was relatively low compared to previous years (LCFP, 2020). Foreign actors were also involved in media activities in Libya. The North Atlantic Treaty Organization (NATO), for example, which helped overthrow the former Libyan president, used social media to identify potential targets and shared this knowledge with opposition actors. One such actor was a Libyan surgeon who left the USA and moved back to Libya to manage a network of contacts including journalists (Ehdeed, 2019, p. 28). This shows that there is often a transnational element to many protest movements occurring inside the region, given, for instance, the sizeable Arab migrant populations in Europe. For instance, the *Hirak* movement in Algeria led to a wave of protests mobilised by the Algerian community in France denouncing France's interventions in Algeria (El-Naggar, 2021, p. 9).

The above examples demonstrate the pressures on Arab journalists who feel trapped in proxy wars across the region. This has prompted many journalists to seek independence from both the state and private media outlets and to set up their own media ventures, mostly with funds from Western media donors.

Journalists as entrepreneurs

One example of such media ventures was *Aswat Masriyya* or Egyptian Voices online news (http://en.aswatmasriya.com), which was set up in the wake of the 2011 uprisings with funds from Thompson

Reuters Foundation, which also helped to fund *Aswat al-Iraq* (or Iraqi Voices) in 2005. Both outlets closed down in 2017 after their funding was discontinued. These links with Western donors, however, usually cause unease in the recipient countries, because the neutrality of the outlets is a matter of concern with questions about whether such Western-funded outlets follow a foreign agenda. For instance, foreign funding in Egypt is looked upon as a tool of the new imperialism that aims to penetrate national security and undermine the government. In Algeria, the authorities blocked a local web-based radio station because it received foreign funding which the government saw as a form of foreign intervention, while in Jordan, the authorities require authorisation from a committee of representatives of the ministries of Interior, Planning, and Trade (Abu Hamad, 2020, pp. 36–7) before receiving funding from abroad.

However, foreign funding may be the only resort for journalists seeking to establish media start-ups due to the monopoly of public and pan-Arab media on the advertising market, coupled with the political factionalism and the use of news media as a means of influencing public opinion in the region (Abu Hamad, 2020, p. 38). This is why several digital media enterprises have been set up in recent years with funding from Western donors. One recent study (Rammal, 2019) provides examples of digital media entrepreneurship in Lebanon, Jordan, and Morocco. In Lebanon, there are approximately 372 online media websites of which the most prominent start-ups are *ArabNet, Step Feed* and *Diwanee, Daraj, Figur-it*, and *Labneh & Facts. Figur-it*, launched in 2016, received funding from overseas in the region of USD 25,000 (Rammal, 2019, p. 13). One of the oldest ventures is ArabNet, launched in 2009, which hosts conferences concerning digital technology, both regionally and globally. *Daraj* online is one of the most recent ventures, launched in 2018 by the veteran Lebanese journalist Diana Moukalled, with funding from a European media development agency. Mokalled argues that foreign subsidy could guarantee independence from local political and financial restrictions, although *Daraj*'s co-founder, Alia Ibrahim contradicts this statement and says that 'even donation money is not independent' (cited in Breiner, 2019). According to one journalist, Western media donors usually target the same 'clique' of Arab journalists who are more likely to receive funding than others with no prior connection to those donors (personal communication, 1 December 2021). Also, no matter how professional the service provided by foreign-subsidised media ventures may be, Arab governments remain sceptical of the potential hidden agenda behind those ventures.

60 *Journalists*

The main concern of such foreign-subsidised outlets is funding which is often unreliable, and it certainly does not match the funding of established pan-Arab outlets or state media. Digital media entrepreneurs have generally identified income uncertainty, great job insecurity, political and economic instability, and lack of skilled labour insecurity as the most pressing challenges, in addition to the harsh competition with content providers outside the region. These ventures, therefore, struggle to generate revenue that guarantees their economic independence, the ability to attract local talent, and find partners to expand regionally and globally (Rammal, 2019, p. 16). Thus, foreign funding is not sustainable, as Diana Mokalled argues, which makes it imperative for such ventures to diversify their income to survive. This is why *Daraj* also provides sponsored content that appeals to some advertisers (Al-Sahafa, 2020, p. 26). There are several other entrepreneurial journalists such as Lina Attalah from *Mada Masr* who received funding from several European donors and had to learn marketing techniques as well as business development skills to promote their work (Breiner, 2019). They also have to be creative in their editorial work to create new streams of income such as providing public relations management and dissemination of information, training and translation services, and, as in the case of *Mada Masr*, subscription-based English-language newsletters for targeted groups (Breiner, 2019). The Tunisian *Inkyfada* is similarly supported by several Western donors including the Open Society Foundation and it depends on non-traditional streams of income including renting out its excess space and offering to create websites for clients for events or training purposes (Breiner, 2019).

In addition, Arab news audiences are usually reluctant to pay for news. *Daraj* founders argue that their outlet has to depend on such donations because 'Arabs won't pay for subscriptions' (cited in Breiner, 2019). Another example is *Ma3azef*, which is the first music e-magazine in the region (ma3azef.com), funded by several Western donors including the International Media Support (IMS), and European Endowment for Democracy. Its founding editor Maan Abu Taleb attributes the problem with financial sustainability to the Arab audience's reluctance to pay for news content, 'Even if Arab readers wanted to financially support the institutions by paying a certain fee to access content, most of them are unable to do so [because means of electronic payment are not common in the Arab world]. We have many readers in Tunisia, most of whom don't have the means to make electronic payments', he said (cited in *Mada Masr*, 2019).

There are also numerous, mostly short-lived, media ventures that have proliferated in the Arab diasporic communities. The Jordanian journalist, Ahmad Abu Hamad, set up a website in Sweden, for example, called *Aylan* in 2018, commemorating the name of Aylan Kurdi, the three-year-old Syrian boy who drowned in the Mediterranean Sea along with his family in September 2015. The website is dedicated to news and information about refugees and immigration. According to Abu Hamad, there is an acute need for such websites to give voice to the refugees as active agents, instead of limiting the media debate between (Western) journalists and policymakers (Hamdou, 2019, p. 15). Another venture in Sweden catering to Arab migrants is *alkompis.se*, launched in 2012; one of its journalists was Qatafa al-Younes, a Syrian-Palestinian man who learned journalism while working on *alkompis*. He later moved to a new Arab media venture in Sweden – *Nabd Oresund* (Oresund Pulse) which faced financial difficulties and was shut down in 2016. According to al-Younes, such Arabic-language media ventures in Europe were unsustainable due to the lack of professional journalists and managers (Hamdou, 2019, pp. 18–19). Another example of refugee journalism is *Campji* (or Campist), a website launched in Lebanon in 2017 to voice the demands of the Arab refugees in Lebanon, which hosts more than 1.5 Syrian and 300,000 Palestinian refugees (Hamdou, 2019, p. 17).

The digital sphere has thus provided new opportunities for journalists and editors to set up new alternative media – often short-lived enterprises – but this begs the question of how this entrepreneurialism has helped journalists upgrade their practices and master new digital tools.

Journalists as technologists

The majority of news institutions in the region suffer from a lack of digitally skilled journalists who can produce multimedia content while mastering traditional news tools and values. One editor told me that journalists still re-produce content from international news agencies such as *Reuters* (personal communication, 10 December 2021). For this editor, the solution for some pan-Arab institutions is to outsource digital content to the so-called 'digital farms' in Egypt so that editors can just decide on the digital content, and then publish and distribute it across various platforms (personal communication, 10 December 2021). However, this solution is not adequate since such farms cannot produce original content. They are more suited to the production of infographics, based on data provided by journalists or editors. Also,

62 *Journalists*

not all newsrooms can afford to outsource digital content, as another journalist said that his newsroom often hires one or two technically competent persons to do the work of a whole team (personal communication, 2 December 2021).

Data journalism is another challenge in Arab newsrooms. The term 'data journalism' is still used with ambiguity to refer to different practices from enriching news with data to using data in large, often collaborative investigative journalism projects (Wright & Doyle, 2018), and sometimes leaked data. In Arab newsrooms, the term is often used to refer to dynamic and static infographics which usually depend on individual journalists' digital skills including the ability to analyse data using spreadsheets. A survey among a sample of Arab journalists (Arab DJN, 2017) showed that only a quarter of journalists used Excel to analyse open data and sought instructions on how to improve their skills in Excel. The majority stated that it was hard to access data on their countries and that they hardly ever used a Freedom of Information request (FOI). One pioneer of Arab data journalism, Amr El-Eraqi, set up *infotimes.org* in 2012 which provided training in data journalism in Arabic. For him, the lack of training in digital journalism motivated him to launch this project. El-Eraqi also said that his venture *Info-times* addressed the need for data journalism in Arab newsrooms by offering new digital content, but it was not profitable:

> *Info-times* began with the idea of offering digital content, but the founders soon abandoned this idea and decided to sell their digital expertise to existing newsrooms instead of competing with those newsrooms. What helped the company to expand was the thirst for data journalism applications in the region, and the need for data visualization in the newsrooms without the need to establish specialised data journalism units.
>
> (El-Eraqi, 2020, p. 23)

There are data journalism workshops, albeit limited in number, in Tunisia, Lebanon, and Algeria (Al-Kaali, 2020, p. 17). One of the trainers of digital journalism was Eva Constantaras who developed a handbook with several cases and translated it into Arabic. Constantaras stresses that digital journalism is not about visualising data but is mostly about critical thinking (cited in Peszkowska, 2019).

Tunisian scholar and trainer, Nouha Belaid (2019), argues that Hackathon events could contribute to developing data journalism practices such as the Data Journalism Hackathon organised in 2017 by the Tunisian Association for E-Governance, for example, as well as the African Centre for Training Journalists and Communication in Tunisia, and *Data4Women* Hackathon organised by Info-Times Foundation in February 2019 in Egypt. There are also individual initiatives such as the one set up by the Yemeni journalist, Muhammad Hizam Al-Fateh, who established the website *Kholassa* (kholassa.com) in 2014, as the first Yemeni website specialising in data journalism. Journalism training in Arab universities needs an overhaul to integrate digital training skills, according to Belaid (2019, p. 31). Belaid recommends hiring new staff specialised in digital training, equipping the universities with the necessary digital tools and software, and establishing lasting cooperation between the faculties of media and IT.

In Western newsrooms, analytic tools like *Chartbeat* are used to track the most 'clickable' articles, in addition to using 'clickbait' headlines, even if they intentionally misrepresent the content of the articles, to drive traffic to them (Christin, 2017). There is a paucity of professionals in Arab newsrooms who master those applications and there is generally a lack of developers to create new journalistic applications. One recent study based on interviews in two state-owned newspapers in Egypt revealed that those who are assigned the development of Augmented Reality and Mixed Reality are seen as a small cohort of professional journalists with special technical skills to develop this kind of technology as required in the newsrooms. The study also showed that Egyptian newsrooms (such as state-owned newspapers) merely imitate the work undertaken in developed countries. This suggests that the experiences of developing countries may be more relevant in identifying how to use such technology to serve local audiences (Abdel Moati, 2020).

Having said that, Arab journalists use 'clickbait' headlines to drive traffic to news websites. According to one Arab journalist (Ezz, 2021), television channels focus on increasing the views on social media sites as the main measurement of their digital success; they tend to entrust digital marketing professionals, not journalists, with social media strategies. The result, according to him, is that many news institutions witness internal conflict between journalists and digital marketers regarding what to produce for digital platforms (Ezz, 2021, p. 58). One solution for digital marketeers to increase the 'Views' and 'Likes' of their channels is to pay *Facebook* and other sites massive sums of money to promote 'sponsored content' for those channels (Ezz, 2021, p. 59). The likes and shares are usually triggered by short, snappy, and entertaining news, as one journalist told me. He mentioned that he often recruits new journalists and producers based on their ability to identify news values for social media sites, namely, short but

64 *Journalists*

entertaining news and picking up snappy headlines for the *Twitter* feed which is usually related to pan-Arab news agendas (personal communication, 5 December 2021). Another means to increase impressions on social media sites is for pan-Arab television channels to rely on live broadcasting of certain segments because live broadcasting tends to attract six times more audiences than recorded videos (Ezz, 2021, p. 60).

The problem with digital training is that journalism education in Arab universities has generally not managed to keep pace with the digital development in the profession. One 2017 survey of 439 courses in the fields of communication, media, and journalism, offered by 120 universities and educational institutions in nine Arab countries, revealed a gap between theory and practice, and a lack of material about digital journalism and digital methods, in addition to the shortage of academics specialised in digital media (Al-Raji, 2020, p. 40). A survey among media students as well as journalists in the GCC states exploring their view on journalism curricula showed dissatisfaction with those curricula which tend to discount practical elements in favour of a theoretical approach (Ziani et al., 2018). Seven universities in Jordan teach journalism, but there is a general skills gap between what is taught theoretically at these universities and the practical needs of newsrooms. There is also a shortage of teachers with practical professional experience. The result is that the unemployment rate among journalism and media graduates exceeds 65 per cent, except for those who obtained their degrees from Jordan Media Institute with its limited graduates of 40 annually (*USAID*, 2020, pp. 6–7). Also, some practical subjects such as data visualisation and photojournalism may not be adequately taught in universities, but rather through informal apprenticeships. In Egypt, for instance, a study on selected newspapers shows the lack of using data visualisation to simplify complex information, while other newspapers such as *Al-Masry al-Youm* and *Youm7* confine their digital tools to traditional telecommunication services such as SMS and RSS (Al-Batal, 2018). There is also no training in other skills such as photojournalism, leaving Egyptian photojournalists mostly dependent on apprenticeships with veterans, who, in turn, feel that their role is not recognised in the newsrooms (Ismail, 2020).

Moreover, digital training, such as retrieving and handling data, is not always an attractive subject for many Arab journalism students who perceive a journalist as a broadcaster, television presenter, or war reporter. As such, processing numerical data and mastering Excel functions have nothing to do with journalism for those students; one

Tunisian journalism lecturer (Al-Kaali, 2020, p. 17) comments on this as follows:

> When I ask my students in Tunisia about their ambitions for the future, I hear answers like, 'I want to be a broadcaster, or war reporter or sports journalist' [...] The camera fascinates them, and it is not surprising. They like the camera, they like the radio, and some are still tempted by the press. Journalism, as they see it, is in front of a camera or microphone, and no one is dreaming of spending a big part of their time behind the computer, crunching numbers.

To mitigate the shortage of digital skills inside the newsrooms, some well-resourced pan-Arab media, based in the GCC region, have recently maximised their training budgets to invest in training a new generation of digital media-savvy journalists. The aim is twofold: to maintain the supply of young talent, while engaging with, and appealing to, young people – particularly in the Gulf region – in the growing media market.

Digital training initiatives

Young people in the Gulf region, unlike other Arab nationals, have easier access to the journalistic field, given the high concentration of Gulf investments in the pan-Arab media sector (Mellor, 2011, p. 117). In the past few years, and particularly since the ascension of the Saudi Crown Prince to power in 2015, several digital initiatives have been launched to absorb Saudi young talent to work in the media sector, and to replace Arab expatriates.

Among the new digital academies in the Gulf is the Middle East Broadcasting (MBC) Academy which defines its mission, as stated on its website, as being aimed at showcasing the region's potential, by investing in Saudi youth and serving as 'the first incubator of its kind for Saudi youth to achieve their goals and realise their full potential' and 'to narrate their own stories' (mbcacademy.me). The academy was launched in June 2020 offering Saudi nationals, of both genders aged 18 to 45, training in film, television, radio, digital games, and performing arts. The Academy's graduates are given the opportunity to work across the MBC group which includes MBC Studios, *Shahid*, and contribute to popular talk shows and talent shows. The Academy boasts of training 124 Saudis since its launch, and its ambition is to prepare Saudi young people for opportunities, not only in Saudi media projects but

66 Journalists

also to compete in global competitions such as the Short Film Festival on *TikTok* launched in the Kingdom in 2020 under the auspices of MBC group. There is, in addition, the Saudi Digital Academy (sda.edu.sa) which defines itself as a national initiative to build Saudi digital capabilities in the Kingdom; it boasts of its capacity to train 40,000 Saudi nationals via more than 60 bootcamps and 550 workshops.

Private academies in other GCC states include Sky News Arabia Academy (academy.skynewsarabia.com) in the UAE, as well as *Al-Jazeera* Media Academy (JMA) in Qatar, which is by far the largest academy (institute.aljazeera.net). JMA, in addition to offering short courses in journalism, publishes handbooks about news verification and data journalism. It also provides an e-learning portal with several sessions offered for free, as well as a portal to learn the Arabic language. CNN also recently launched its CNN Academy Abu Dhabi in January 2021, offering insights into *CNN Arabic* and the local media landscape (academy.cnn.com). It should be noted that the majority of CNN courses cost over US$2,000 which means they are not affordable to many budding journalists.

Other academies in the GCC include the *International Media Academy* in Kuwait, *SAE*, *Twofour54*, and *Reporters* in the UAE. *Reporters* is an independent training centre specialising in broadcasting and digital courses; among its proclaimed aims is to fill the 'wide gap between media Faculties' curricula and the requirements of media markets' (reporters.ae/). *Twofour54* in Abu Dhabi (twofour54.com/) is named after the geographic coordinates of Abu Dhabi, aiming to re-brand the Emirate of Abu Dhabi as the capital of content creators; it was launched in 2008, offering customisable office space, production facilities, and talent development training. On its website, it states that it has helped more than 1,000 freelancers, 130+ entrepreneurs, and 5,000+ media professionals.

The ASBU Academy, affiliated with the Arab States Broadcasting Union (ASBU) also offers numerous digital courses, of which the most popular are courses on Cybersecurity, OTT, Augmented Reality in New Media, AI applications, and IP-based television studios. However, these technical courses, according to the Academy's website, are aimed at technicians and engineers, while basic data journalism and traditional courses in news values are offered primarily to journalists, reporters, and producers.

In my view, Arab digital journalistic practices are still confined to using social media sites to find trending stories, rather than gathering data from databanks. Following what is trendy on social media sites is, for many journalists, a means of satisfying young audiences' needs for fast news. For instance, one online journalist considers digital journalism to be about trends online as well as digital marketing tools (personal communication, 28 August 2021). Trends, in this case, include familiarisation with the latest apps available to media professionals. Attractive and trendy stories, such as in Egypt, include human-interest stories attributed to audiences' desire to see more news stories and features that represent their daily problems, often discussed on social media sites (Jamal, 2021). This trend, however, is usually pertinent to certain genres of information (infotainment), and not necessarily to political or economic news, save for specialised (propaganda-like) outlets, whether set up by states or non-state actors.

Conclusion

One solution for developing the journalistic field and gearing it to the digital sphere, according to one journalist, is to encourage profit-driven news institutions which can raise funds, whether through users' subscriptions or advertising, remote from the control of states or crony businessmen (personal communication, 28 August 2021). Lack of funding is undoubtedly a hindrance in the Arab region, and there is an acute need to identify new business models which can sustain the numerous existing outlets. There is moreover an acute need for digitally skilled journalists equipped to navigate their paths in the high-tech realm. In addition to these digital tools, journalists (as well as other professionals) are expected to master English, which has become the lingua franca of an increasingly technological world (As-Shawabka, 2021, p. 69).

Overall, the Arab journalism field has witnessed major transformations since the emergence of social media sites. These have given rise to new types of media personalities, namely, young bloggers, and later citizen journalists and even influencers. This new generation of media figures has attracted much public attention, prompting newsrooms to acknowledge the power of this new digital media-savvy generation. Professional journalists, nonetheless, see the difference between them and social media personalities centring on news values: A professional journalist can identify news relevant to Arab audiences while being able to communicate it succinctly on social media sites. On the other hand, several conflict-ridden countries witnessed an explosion of Western-funded media outlets in the first phases of the conflict, as was the case in Iraq (post-2003), Syria, Yemen, and Libya (post-2011), as well as a rise in online citizen journalism, many of which were ideologically biased by focusing on discrediting their political opposition

68 *Journalists*

(Aït Mous & Ksikes, 2018). The outcome has been a more complex media landscape, with hundreds of outlets disseminating a handful of, rather than diverse, opinions due to the entanglement of journalism and politics.

This saturated Arab media and news market means that journalists have also found themselves competing for audiences' attention with bloggers, citizen journalists, and social media influencers who have amassed a huge number of followers, as we will see in the next chapter.

References

Abdel Moati, Hind Yahya A. (2020) Use of Augmented Reality and Mixed Reality Technology in Online Press (in Arabic). *The Egyptian Journal of Public Opinion Research*, Vol. 19(2), Spring 2020, pp. 35–109.

Abu Hamad, Ahmad (2020) Foreign Subsidies: New Imperialism or the Key to the Missing Independence, December 21, 2020, Al-Jazeera Media Institute, https://institute.aljazeera.net/en/node/1324

Aït Mous, Fadma & Driss Ksikes (2018) The Life Span of Alternative Media: Cases of Lakome and Mamfakinch in Morocco, Jadaliyya, March 29, 2018, https://www.jadaliyya.com/Print/36378

Al-Abdallah, Mai, Haytham Qotb & Majid Turban (eds.) (2017) Tools of Communications and Social Awareness in the Arab World (in Arabic). Arab Association for Research and Communication Sciences (AARCS).

Al-Batal, Hani Ibrahim (2018) Elements of Egyptian E-newspaper Design. *Arab Media & Communication Research journal*, Issue 20, January–March 2018, pp. 4–43 (in Arabic).

Al-Hefnawy, Mohamed (2014) Media and Development in the Globalisation Age (in Arabic), Desouk: Dar Al-Ilm wal Iman, p. 5.

Alhussein, Eman (2019) Saudi First: How Hyper-Nationalism Is Transforming Saudi Arabia, Policy Brief June 2019, https://ecfr.eu/publication/saudi_first_how_hyper_nationalism_is_transforming_saudi_arabia/

Al-Kaali, Arwa (2020) Why Do We Fear Teaching Data Journalism? (in Arabic), *Al-Sahafa*, Vol. 5(20), Winter 2020, pp. 16–21.

Allam, Rasha (2019) Constructive Journalism in Arab Transitional Democracies: Perceptions, Attitudes and Performance, *Journalism Practice*, Vol. 13(10), pp. 1273–93.

Al-Raji, Mohamad (ed.) (2020) *The Environment of Arab Online Press-Contexts and Challenges* (in Arabic). Doha: Al-Jazeera Centre for Studies

Al-Sahafa (2020) Interview with Diana Mokalled, Vol. 5(19) (in Arabic), https://institute.aljazeera.net/ar/ajr/article/1344

Al-Sharq al-Awsat (2021, Mar. 25) A Media Professor Accused of Insulting Media Professionals, (in Arabic), https://bit.ly/3B7FoNt

Arab DJN (2017) Data Journalism in The Arab World. Survey Results, July–October 2017. Cairo: Arab DJN

Journalists 69

Arabi21 (2019, Nov. 28) Egyptian Officials Respond to Hashim Qasim, (in Arabic), https://bit.ly/3LaWQFw

As-Shawabka, Mosab (2021) Review of a Book About Moroccan Press and Ideology. *Al-Sahafa*, Vol. 6(21), Spring 2021, (in Arabic), pp. 64–75.

Badr, Hanan (2020) The Egyptian Syndicate and (Digital) Journalism's Unresolved Boundary Struggle, *Digital Journalism*, DOI: 10.1080/21670811.2020.1799424

Bazon, Ahmad (2017) The Crisis of Lebanese Press. *Al-Faisal Magazine*, June 30, 2017, (in Arabic), https://www.alfaisalmag.com/?p=5448

Belaid, Nouha (2019) *Data Journalism Handbook*. Tunis: Tunisia E-Gov Society.

Benchenna, Abdelfettah & Dominique Marchetti (2020) Writing Between the 'Red Lines': Morocco's Digital Media Landscape. *Media, Culture & Society*, DOI: 10.1177/0163443720972316

Breiner, James (2019) How Necessity Drives Media Innovation in Middle East, North Africa. *Global Investigative Journalism Network*, January 3, 2019, https://gijn.org/2019/01/03/how-necessity-drives-media-innovation-in-middle-east-north-africa/

Christin, Angele (2017) Algorithms in Practice: Comparing Web Journalism and Criminal Justice, *Big Data & Society*, DOI: 10.1177/2053951717718855

Cockburn, Patrick (2017) Who Supplies the News? *LRB*, Vol. 39(3), February 2, 2017, https://www.lrb.co.uk/the-paper/v39/n03/patrick-cockburn/who-supplies-the-news

Ehdeed, Skina (2019) *The Emergence of Libyan Networked Publics: Social Media Use Before, During and After the Libyan Uprising*. Unpublished PhD thesis, The University of Sheffield, UK.

El-Eraqi, Amr (2020) Infotimes – Arabic Platform Story I Believed in Data Journalism, *Al-Sahafa*, Vol. 5(20), Winter 2020, (in Arabic), pp. 22–7.

El-Naggar, Linda (2021) The Return of the Hirak Movement and the June Legislative Elections: What Path for Algeria? The Swedish Institute of International Affairs, Policy brief, 4/2021.

Ezz, Ammar (2021) TV as a Follower for Social Media. *Al-Sahafa Magazine*, Vol 6(21), Spring 2021, (in Arabic). Doha: Al-Jazeera Media Institute, pp. 58–63.

Fikry, Amira (2019) Egyptian Politicians Recruit Marketing Companies as Their Spokespersons (in Arabic). *Al-Arab*, Vol. 42(11542), November 18, 2019, p. 18.

Hafez, Ahmad (2021) Egypt without Private Media. *Al-Arab*, March 19, 2021, Vol. 43(12004), (in Arabic), p. 1, https://bit.ly/3ibXcQg

Hamdou, Ahmad Haj (2019) Refugee Journalism. *Al-Sahafa Magazine*, Vol. 4(15) (in Arabic). Doha: Al-Jazeera Media Institute.

IFEX (2021) Palestine: Rights Groups Condemn Cyberespionage Operations, April 23, 2021, https://ifex.org/palestine-rights-groups-condemn-cyberespionage-operations/

70 *Journalists*

Ismail, Fathi Ibrahim (2020) Obstacles to the Practice of Photojournalism in the Egyptian Press (in Arabic). *Arab Media & Communication Research,* Issue 30, July–September 2020, pp. 366–418.

Jamal, Ahmad (2021) Human-Interest Stories in the Egyptian Media Restore Journalists' Relationship with the Audience. *Al-Arab,* Septemebr 25, 2021, (in Arabic), https://bit.ly/3GvMpsD

Kozman, Claudia & Raluca Cozma (2021) Keeping the Gates on Twitter: Interactivity and Sourcing Habits of Lebanese Traditional Media, *International Journal of Communication,* Vol. 15, pp. 1000–20.

LCFP (2020) Libya's Journalists Are a Road Full of Danger and Violence. Annual report 2018–19, Libyan Center for Freedom of Press/LCFP, May 2019, www.LCFP.org.ly

Mada Masr (2019, May 4) How Do We Continue? How Do We Make an Impact? https://www.madamasr.com/en/2019/05/04/feature/society/how-do-we-continue-how-do-we-make-an-impact/

Meghawer, Mohamed (2018), Raising the Price of Newspapers (in Arabic). *Arabi21,* August 9, https://bit.ly/2rKfxvG

Mellor, Noha (2005) *The Making of Arab News.* Lanham, MD: Rowman & Littlefield.

Mellor, Noha (2007) *Modern Arab Journalism.* Edinburgh: Edinburgh University Press.

Mellor, Noha (2011) *Arab Journalists in pan-Arab Media.* New York: Hampton Press.

Omar, Ahmad (2020) Osama Heikal Faces Criticism and Calls for His Resignation. *BBC Arabic,* October 20, 2020, https://www.bbc.com/arabic/middleeast-54614788

Peszkowska, Alicja (2019) Interview with Eva Constantaras, Medium, April 25, 2019, https://medium.com/outriders/i-use-the-hype-of-data-journalism-as-a-pretext-to-teach-the-fundamentals-of-public-interest-f51adc3ed60e

Rammal, Ali (2019) Digital Media Startup Companies in the Arab World. The Examples of Lebanon, Morocco and Jordan. Maharat Foundation. http://maharatfoundation.org/media/1810/digital-media-startup-companies-in-the-arab-world-2019.pdf

Robinson, Piers (2019) War and Media since 9/11, *European Journal of Communication,* Vol. 34(5), pp. 557–63.

Shehabat, Ahmad (2013) The Social Media Cyber-War: The Unfolding Events in the Syrian Revolution 2011, *Global Media Journal* (Australian edition), July 2013, https://www.semanticscholar.org/paper/The-social-media-cyber-war-%3A-the-unfolding-events-Shehabat/529f793582abc72581d-0b0696483972abeb28d5e

Shupak, Gregory (2018) Media Erase US Role in Syria's Misery, Call for US to Inflict More Misery, fair.org, March 7, 2018, https://fair.org/home/media-erase-us-role-in-syrias-misery-call-for-us-to-inflict-more-misery/

The Syrian Centre for Media and Freedom of Expression (2021) Syria: The Black Hole for Media Work-10 Years of Violations. May 2021, https://scm.bz/en/en-studies/syria-the-black-hole-for-media-work-eng

USAID (2020) Jordan Media Assessment, June 9, 2020, https://pdf.usaid.gov/pdf_docs/PA00WQVH.pdf

Wright, Scott & Kim Doyle (2018): The Evolution of Data Journalism: A Case Study of Australia, *Journalism Studies*, DOI: 10.1080/1461670X.2018.1539343.

Ziani, Abdul-Karim, Mokhtar Elareshi, Maha Alrashid & Khalid Al-Jaber (2018) Journalism Education in the GCC Region: University Students' and Professionalism Perspectives, *Media Watch*, Vol. 9 (1), pp. 52–68, DOI: 10.15655/mw/2018/v9i1/49275

Note

1 The group was designated as a terrorist organisation in 2013 by the UN Security Council.

4 Audiences

Introduction

It is often argued that social media has accelerated the role of audiences who challenge the traditional gatekeeping role of professional journalists, not only by amplifying certain stories but also by providing more information unavailable in mainstream media. The new opportunities to speak out online have produced several instances of the suppression of various young voices on social media platforms. Examples abound and include a young Jordanian man who was deported from Kuwait after protesting against the authorities' action on unvaccinated people. The decision resulted in a *Twitter* campaign, '#No to deportation', to demand the reversal of this decision because he was only practising his right to express his views (*Al-Arab*, 2021b, July 1). There were also several young women in Egypt who were arrested and fined for violating moral values on their *TikTok* and *Instagram* posts (Osman, 2021).

This chapter zooms in on Arab audiences, especially young people's use of digital media to access information and news, shedding new light on youth's distrust of news media, the proliferation of misinformation and disinformation on the Internet, and the rise of the so-called 'citizen journalism' as a channel for accessing the journalistic field. Social media have provided an avenue for fame and financial success for some groups of audiences which is especially illustrated by the rise of 'social media influencers' in the Arab region.

This chapter begins with a brief discussion of the distrust of news media, particularly among young Arabs, which may justify the audience's reluctance to pay for or subscribe to the news online, and it continues with an exploration of the attitudes and behaviour of audiences regarding social media.

DOI: 10.4324/9781003218838-5

Young audiences

Several Arab states have seen new patterns of media usage, in which social media have become the number one source of news for youth, overtaking television, according to the Arab Youth Survey 2020 (arabyouthsurvey.com). The growing segment of young audiences has led to an increased need for on-demand streaming content, whether over-the-top (OTT) or video-on-demand (VOD) content. *Netflix* has consequently expanded its operation in MENA, while Telecom operators have joined this new market by launching their own initiatives such as *eLife ON* in the UAE and *Mosaic* in Qatar (IPSOS, 2017, p. 2). The largest VOD provider is *MBC Shahid.net*, owned by the Saudi conglomerate MBC group. MBC also owns *MBC Mobile Services* and *MBC Studios*, as well as channels catering to audiences in Egypt (*MBC Misr*), Morocco (*MBC5*), and Iraq (*MBC Iraq*). The VOD Shahid was rebranded in 2020 under the slogan 'it's our time', marking a new phase of original Arabic content produced and distributed via MBC (Khalil & Zayani, 2021). Another leading broadcaster in the region is *Orbit Showtime Network* (OSN) which is a direct-broadcast channel, specialising in entertainment, most of which is based on 'Arabised' versions of American and British content. OSN introduced *OSN play* in 2012 – an online and VOD platform. The company announced that it recorded a 200 per cent increase in the number of viewers of its content, especially during the peak of COVID-19 in 2020. This trend encouraged *OSN* to plan a 25 per cent increase in its Arabic content by the end of 2021, according to its CEO, Patrick Tillieux (cited in Al-Zayyani, 2021):

> Satellite broadcasting continues to be of value and importance in the region, as accessing a robust broadband Internet infrastructure can be a challenge in some parts of the region. We cannot ignore the presence of large segments of the public that can only access television channels through satellite dishes [...]; although the number of online audiences is increasing, satellite channels will not disappear anytime soon.

It is important to note that original Arabic-language drama is rather costly and can total more than USD200,000 per episode, which has prompted many television stations to rely on foreign series (in Turkish, English, or Hindi) and dubbing them into Arabic to lower the cost to an average of USD3,000 per hour (EY, 2018, p. 18). The result is a slow increase in Arabic-language content due to its high cost.

74　*Audiences*

Generally, most audiences prefer free services in Arabic, even if it means exposure to heavy advertising, although a smaller group would subscribe to *OTT* content piecemeal. Audiences in poorer Arab states, on the other hand, tend to avoid paying for subscription-based content. They notoriously resorted to developing piracy practices by using unauthorised decoders or connecting an entire block of flats to one paid subscription (Khalil & Zayani, 2021).

The majority of Arab audiences, however, are reluctant to pay for news online, preferring to pay for entertainment and sports only. IPSOS surveys show that audiences in selected states (Egypt, Saudi Arabia, and the UAE) were prepared to pay for *OTT*, particularly entertainment such as films (38 per cent of respondents), sports (34 per cent), TV drama (25 per cent), and music (24 per cent), but only 10 per cent paid for news content (IPSOS, 2017, p. 6). Another audience survey among a random sample of 530 people in the UAE, Saudi Arabia, and Oman, showed the audience's reluctance to pay for news, and they were largely uninterested in following subscription-based online news – even foreign sites – although they were willing to pay for films or music (Darwich & Younes, 2020). When it comes to news, audiences prefer free content, and this trend is unlikely to change in the future. The irony is that news apps tend to record more visits than entertainment apps, especially with breaking news which has led some *OTT* services to use the news to drive traffic to their apps (EY, 2018, p. 42). One editor told me that subscription-based news is the only viable model in the future, and it will eventually force newsrooms to invest in good journalism to attract more subscribers. He also mentioned the examples of the Kuwaiti *Al-Qabas* and the Lebanese *Al-Nahar* which run some premium services online and he expects other news outlets to follow suit in the next five years. He referred to how *Shahid* had attracted many subscribers; although, as he said, when it began, no one believed that Arab users would pay for it, until the launch of *Netflix* (personal communication, 1 December 2021). This prediction, however, is not shared by others in the field because news channels, as one journalist argued, want to attract audiences to their [ideological] content, and so content must be made available for free, because these channels do not seek profit, but influence (personal communication, 2 December 2021).

Social media platforms, moreover, have pushed Arab newsrooms to prioritise audience segmentation, and to compete in offering soft news, depending on the platform; for instance, Twitter will be used for hard news, whereas Facebook for visuals and entertaining news (Ayish & Mellor, 2015, p. 57). This means that several Arab media

Audiences 75

outlets have partnered with social media platforms to maximise their reach. The Saudi-owned *MBC TV* channel, for example, entered into a partnership with *Facebook* to share content, including the *Ramadan* series for 2021, while *Nestle Middle East* created a bot for *Facebook Messenger*, and partnered with *Zenith MENA* and *Chatlab* to create a bilingual, English and Arabic bot. *Facebook* also partnered with several entertainment providers in the region, as well as social media influencers. It joined *Al-Ghad* TV, launched in 2012 in London, to promote a new show hosted by the Egyptian journalist Ibrahim Eissa. The channel ran 15-second and 30-second video ads to promote the show on *Facebook* and used analytics to focus on the reach and impressions.[1]

Twitter also saw growth in online video consumption in the MENA region. This prompted a further expansion of its activities in MENA, but with individualised campaigns for each country. The *Twitter* MENA director, Benjamin Ampen explained:

> The effort and initiatives we need to push in Egypt are different to the ones in Saudi, where *Twitter* has become a utility [...]. This is a region where we need to choose our battles, and the battles are different depending on the country
>
> (cited in Townsend, 2018).

Twitter activities usually focus on video marketing content placed on its accounts, and building chat programmes to engage audiences. These campaigns are ultimately used to measure Return on Investment (ROI) compared to campaigns on legacy media. To obtain this ROI, social media campaigns must aim to micro-target users based on their online profiles such as occupation, gender, education, interests, and so on. *Twitter* in Saudi Arabia, for instance, claims that its ads are 20 per cent more effective than other ad formats (*Twitter*, n.d.).

Social media users, on the other hand, may impose their own hierarchy on the news by following some stories while neglecting others (Harlow & Kilgo, 2021). This means that biases in the offline communication sphere may be replicated and reinforced on digital platforms. This also means that mainstream journalists who actively follow users' engagement as an indication of newsworthiness, may end up legitimising certain events by favourably covering them instead of others, depending on the public support they received. This trend ultimately has an impact on the news media's reliability, especially with the declining trust in Arab news media.

76 *Audiences*

Distrusting the news

Global surveys of trust in the news media indicate that levels in the Arab region are declining, with an IPSOS survey showing that respondents' trust in television and radio is only 61 per cent, followed by the press at 59 per cent, and online sites at 58 per cent, while their trust in people they know is 65 per cent. People's perceived prevalence of fake news is highest when it comes to online websites (56 per cent), followed by broadcasting (53 per cent) and the press (51 per cent) (Chalmers, 2019, p. 7). During crises, audiences nonetheless seem to flock to digital platforms. During the peak of COVID-19 in 2020, for instance, there was an increase in fake news on social media, and yet Arab audiences expressed more confidence in the information posted on *Twitter, YouTube,* and *WhatsApp*, than on *Facebook* which many considered as a hub for fake news (Khalifa et al., 2020). On the other hand, legacy media including newspapers, television, and radio are losing their credibility, as digital platforms and their algorithms are perceived as more neutral. A recent survey among UAE internet users, for example, argued that Emiratis tend to trust algorithms more than American users (Shin, Chotiyaputta & Zaid, 2021).

The level of trust, however, varies across the region. In Jordan, for instance, new media suffer from a lack of credibility with more and more Jordanians indicating that they did not trust information circulating online, with one survey confirming this low level of trust in new and social media (*USAID*, 2020). Trust in governmental portals and digital initiatives also varied: An app was launched by the Jordanian Prime Minister in 2018 called 'At Your Service' where citizens could file complaints and send questions to the government. Another app was launched in the same year, under the name 'Your Right to Know' to combat fake news. Users were asked to verify the information before sharing it on social media; however, most users did not download the apps or use the online forms (*USAID*, 2020, p. 5). On the other hand, some Jordanians prefer to follow international television believing that this may be less biased in covering certain political controversies, such as the dispute within the royal family between the king and his brother in 2021, which was not covered by Jordanian media (*IFEX*, 2021a). Also, social media platforms have lost some of their credibility among civil society groups, not only due to the inability of these platforms to monitor disinformation, but also their reluctance to grant access to tools such as *CrowdTangle* to civil society groups (Elswah & Howard, 2020).

Audiences 77

In Tunisia, surveys reveal declining trust in news media. A public opinion survey (Zogby Research, 2018) conducted in eight Arab states showed that Arab audiences' trust in media was only 10 per cent in Tunisia, 28 per cent in Egypt, and 23 per cent in Iraq, compared to a massive 80 per cent in both Saudi Arabia and the UAE. Another survey among a sample of citizens in Tunisia (Sigma, 2020) showed that the media were among the least trusted (46 per cent) along with the government (26 per cent), and the parliament (11 per cent). On the other hand, trust in the army was the highest (96 per cent) – even higher than the president (70 per cent), and clerics (51 per cent). The survey also showed that Tunisians tended to prefer local media (81 per cent) to pan-Arab ones (17 per cent). It is worth mentioning, however, that there is a variation between Arab states when it comes to foreign news, depending on the size of expatriates. One study of the front-page stories of Kuwait Times between 2017 and 2019 revealed that international news stories were more prevalent than local ones (Onyebadi & Satti, 2021), and this could be justified by the large expatriate community residing in Kuwait.

The Sigma (2020) survey also showed that *Al-Jazeera*, once the leading channel reporting on the 2011 uprisings in Tunisia, Egypt, Yemen, and Syria, had lost some of its share of audience since 2011. The same argument was made about the perception of *Al-Jazeera Arabic* in Libya, where the channel was claimed to have lost part of its credibility as a neutral source of information in Libya (Ehdeed, 2019). Another reason for distrusting legacy media is its tendency to disseminate stereotypes rather than to be appealing to disabled audiences. According to Silvana Lakis, President of an NGO that promotes the rights of disabled people in the region, it is hypocritical of some Arab news outlets to claim that they are 'the voice of all people' (which is *Al-Jazeera*'s motto) when they do not even hire disabled journalists (cited in Majzoub, 2021, p. 23). This is unfortunate, Lakis said, as disabled Arab groups are considered the 'largest minority' in a region plagued by wars and conflicts (cited in Majzoub, 2021, pp. 24–6).

Arab audiences also expressed different views when asked about their perception of freedom of speech in their countries. One opinion poll about the perception of freedom of expression and press granted in Arab countries demonstrated more positive responses than expected. Approximately 55 per cent of Egyptians believed that freedom of expression and the press were more or less guaranteed in Egypt, compared to 60 per cent in Algeria, and ca. 75 per cent in Jordan (*Arab* Barometer, 2018). As for access to information, ca.

78 *Audiences*

63 per cent of Egyptian respondents declared that they had not even tried to access blocked information, compared to 31 per cent of Saudi respondents.

In summary, young peoples' dissatisfaction is reflected in polls documenting the level of (mis)trust in media in comparison with other institutions. The increasing distrust in legacy media, coupled with the political shake-ups since 2011 has led to the emergence of a new category of journalists, namely citizen journalists, referring particularly to activists-cum-journalists who disseminate news and views online, either as individual commentators or as budding journalists. Another category of digital users has also emerged, the so-called 'social media influencers', who often create entertaining, but rather superficial content merely to amass a large follower base. The following sections discuss each of these two categories.

Citizen journalists

There were several activists and protestors who used digital media to report and document their protests and atrocities on the ground in the wake of the 2011 uprisings. This marked the rise of the 'citizen journalists', whose style of reporting often blurred the boundaries between witnessing and staging events (Al-Ghazzi, 2014). Post-2011, and with the sharp focus on the role of social media in mobilising Arab youth, several news outlets recruited social media influencers as online journalists whose professionalism left much to be desired by traditional journalists. There were some of these 'citizen journalists' who joined mainstream newspapers, and were given the responsibility for following the debates on social media and readers' emails to assess the value of citizens' stories; the majority were related to problems in education, health, and housing sectors (Sobeih, 2019, p. 416). According to the editor of *al-Youm7* in Egypt, for instance, his newspaper was a pioneer in citizen journalism which he defined as the news and photos received by readers and edited by professional journalists (Sobeih, 2019). The editor provided the example of the suicide attack that targeted a mosque in Kuwait in 2015; the photographs were taken by a Kuwaiti citizen and shared with the newspaper. Some contributors asked for awards or certificates in recognition of their work, and in rare cases, they were financially rewarded, according to the same editor (cited in Sobeih, 2019, p. 410).

The civil wars and turbulent situation in Libya, Yemen, Syria, and Iraq, have also led hundreds of citizens of those countries to the field

Audiences 79

of journalism through volunteering as 'citizen journalists'. One example is Fadi al-Halabi, a Syrian young man from the city of Aleppo, who said,

> I entered the field of media in conjunction with the start of the demonstrations in Aleppo, the absence of journalists, and the falsification of facts [...] I did not expect my work to spread. My dream was to appear on television, and after two years of working in the field of photography, I took training in the media, especially photography, and developed my work to provide distinctive content different from that shown on social media.
>
> (cited in Namous, 2018, p. 24).

Two years later, al-Halabi joined the French Agency (AFP) and broadcast several reports on local Syrian and Arab channels, as well as international outlets such as *BBC, CNN,* and *TRT.* It was important for al-Halabi to report on the Syrian regime, by producing documentaries about the situation in Syria. Al-Halabi won second place in the 'Rory Pack' festival for the best War photographer, and contributed to the filming of 'The Last Men in Aleppo'; he was nominated for an Oscar in 2018. Another example is the Iraqi Asad al-Zalzali, who began as a citizen journalist in Baghdad in 2004 before he joined several newsrooms as a professional journalist (Namous, 2018, p. 26).

Displaced Syrians in refugee camps have also set up their own news ventures. Syrian refugees in Lebanon set up the *Campji* website with a group of young Syrians who created genuine content from the refugee camps. Their declared aim was to transfer the reality of refugees by giving them a voice. The initiative also owns a *YouTube* channel and is also present on *Facebook.* It showcases stories of displaced Syrians and their dreams of a better future.[2] A group of four Syrian journalists who fled to Spain similarly set up a refugee-led news site called *Baynana* (Between Us), which publishes news in both Arabic and Spanish to cater to the Arabic-speaking refugee community in Spain (Dzhanova, 2021).

There are several examples of citizen journalists in Yemen such as A'seel Sariyya who joined the profession in 2007 and became a member of the European-funded *ARIJ* network where he received training in investigative reporting, in 2015. One of his investigative pieces was about humanitarian aid in Yemen, proving the manipulation by donor organisations; in another investigation, he proved the discrimination and deprivation that many segments of Yemenis

80 *Audiences*

face in the labour market (Namous, 2018, p. 27). Another example from Libya is Moataz, who earned a degree in English Literature, and worked in the tourism sector until the 2011 uprising which brought the whole sector to a halt. He then worked as a correspondent for several English-language online outlets until 2013, when he obtained a contract from *Libya Herald*.

A plethora of citizen journalists and original content creators have proliferated post-2011 – some work in state-supported ventures, while others are considered as political opposition. A website called 'The Arab Podcast', ar-podcast.com, set up in 2017 by a Saudi podcaster, hosts a collection of selected podcasts by young Arabs. The site hosted 427 active podcasts at the time of writing, whereas 448 other podcasts were discontinued. The site claims more than 2,800 podcaster and subscriber members. Its declared aim is to increase the number of podcasts in Arabic because Arabic-language content is still limited. Another podcast is the Saudi-based *Mstdfr* Network, mstdfr.com, aiming to serve as a platform for Arab podcasters to share their content. It hosts shows on a range of topics including business, culture, and entertainment.

On the other hand, political opposition podcasters include 'The Arab Tyrant Manual' arabtyrantmanual.com set up by the Palestinian Iyad el-Baghdadi, who was born in Kuwait and raised in the UAE. His *Tweets* about the Egyptian uprisings, and ridiculing the region's dictators prompted his arrest. The site justifies its presence by the rise of right-wing extremism around the world, which peaked with the election of Trump, as stated on the website (arabtyrantmanual.com). There are other examples of such political podcasters such as Ahmed Gatnash, a British-Libyan activist, and co-founder of the *Kawaakibi* Foundation; Khalid al-Baih, a Sudanese political cartoonist based in Copenhagen, and Sana Sekkarie, a researcher of the Syrian conflict.

Citizen journalists are unlikely to be recognised as professional journalists trained in verifying and authenticating news. One study among a sample of journalists covering Syria, Libya, Yemen, and Iraq from neighbouring countries showed how professional reporters set the boundaries that separate them from citizen journalists. The study (Christensen & Khalil, 2021) included a sample of reporters and video producers who worked for international outlets such the *CNN*, the *Associated Press*, *Wall Street Journal*, *Reuters*, *AFP*, and *Al-Arabiya* channel. This cohort of journalists mostly agrees that the journalism field still needs their professional input to filter and verify information which amateur or citizen journalists do not or are unable to do. One

Audiences 81

journalist highlighted the professional journalists' ability to discern reliable from unreliable sources:

> Sometimes, the parties, or even residents, post video and news that is fabricated or in favour of one side. Here, as a journalist, you contact the sources and verify the authenticity of the video. There are many of these videos and statements that we don't use after they appear on social media. Some pages and accounts are fake, [even] using the names of officials. We have to verify the account and page [...]. Sometimes I need to call more than one official to verify a post, asking if [he or she] posted the statement. Sometimes, the story gets delayed until we verify what has been posted on social media.
>
> (cited in Christensen & Khalil, 2021, p. 11).

Citizen journalism, according to another Syrian citizen journalist, emerged because it was a cheap option for news outlets which were happy to use the material provided by amateurs. Absi Sumaisem, who works for *Al-Araby al-Jade*ed (owned by Qatar and based in London), agreed that using activists or amateurs instead of professional journalists is indeed an economic option:

> There were large media outlets that relied on activists and amateurs, and were able to select the most 'professional' of them, but this issue affected the credibility of the media that worked in countries of conflict and countries of the Arab Spring. There are many amateur journalists, who, despite their professional tools, are committed to their revolutions, and thus cannot be objective in their reports.
>
> (cited in Namous, 2018, p. 29).

Newsrooms are therefore usually reluctant to recognise these service providers as professional journalists and do not offer them any training or long-term contracts. A local outlet in Turkey, for instance, depended on 30 Syrian citizen journalists to provide material but did not offer them work contracts (Al-Qutly, 2018, p. 6).

Citizen journalists are also not offered any legal protection which exposes them to various legal and direct risks (Haider, 2018, p. 11). Citizen journalists are also claimed to be damaging the journalism profession. That is why some political and economic elites seek to control and influence the reporting of these amateur journalists. One example is a professional Palestinian journalist who wrote a piece revealing

82 *Audiences*

the rotten food served in a restaurant in Palestine. This prompted the restaurant owner to hire other, more famous, citizen journalists to write positive posts about his restaurant (Shehada, 2018, p. 37). Reporters working with Western media outlets in conflict-ridden countries such as Iraq were often persecuted as traitors working for the USA and its allies during the occupation; when ISIS seized large swathes of land, it too prosecuted several local and foreign reporters such as the Iraqi female journalist Suha Radi who was beheaded in July 2015 (Christensen & Khalil, 2021).

Social media influencers

Social media platforms have also witnessed the rise of the so-called Arab social media influencers in addition to online activists and citizen journalists. *YouTube* has seen the rise of many individual users who have become digital celebrities such as the Canada-based Syrian couple, Anas and Asala whose *YouTube* channel has 12 million followers and growing.[3] There is also *EyshElly* channel[4], featuring a Saudi comedian who has more than three million subscribers, and *Sa7i* Channel[5] (entertainment) with over three and a half million followers. It is worth noting that *YouTube* is the most popular social media platform in the UAE with 8.65 million users (*Global Media Insight*, 2021).

Indeed, Dubai has become the capital of social media influencers in the region. The Turkish influencer Busra Duran moved to Dubai in 2019, arguing that Dubai is the place for big brands. The UAE influencer Taim al-Falasi is one of the influencers on *Snapchat* with more than three million followers; she is reported to charge up to £3,000 for a single photograph (*JWT Intelligence*, 2021). The rise of these influencers has prompted a Dubai-based university to introduce a social media influencer diploma, taught over eight months, and aimed at targeting established and budding influencers (Rizvi, 2019). These social media influencers tend to act as brand ambassadors for international companies such as cosmetics or clothing outlets, taking advantage of their large number of followers. The hospitality sector in Dubai has supported social media influencers to not only promote their brands, but also Dubai as a tourist destination. Influencers in the UAE range from small-scale operators such as students who do this promotional work in their spare time, to established practitioners who do it as a lifestyle. The rise of those influencers has led the UAE government to regulate the work of social media influencers. The UAE authorities now require a trade licence amounting to around USD 4,000 per year. Those who fail to comply with this regulation, risk a fine of more than

Audiences 83

USD1,000; in 2018, more than 500 licences were issued, and in 2019, the number jumped to 1,700 (Gibbs, 2020).

In Egypt, too, social media influencers have amassed millions of followers; it is worth noting that it is not unusual to quickly amass half a million followers on a new *YouTube* channel, in a populous country such as Egypt. These influencers share daily experiences about lifestyle, using products, comedy, or DIY activities (Ezzat, 2020). Their content is usually centred on the mundane life of the creator such as an Egyptian couple, Hamdy and Wafaa, who have more than four million subscribers to their *YouTube* channel, while another 'vlogger' couple, Ahmed Hassan and his wife Zeinab boast more than six million followers of their *YouTube* channel. There is also an abundance of fake accounts in Egypt. Many young people are blamed for using fake accounts of celebrities to establish acquaintances with women, and asking for private photographs which can later be used for blackmail. One Egyptian nutritionist also claimed that she was shocked by an account attributed to her with tens of thousands of followers where women clients are asked to send naked photographs of themselves to identify the best treatment for weight loss (Al-Arab, 2021, Sept. 4).

In addition to fashionista and lifestyle influencers, Muslim preachers also amass millions of followers such as the Egyptian Mustafa Hosny (with more than five million subscribers on *YouTube*). On the other hand, the digital sphere has also given space to opposing voices such as non-believers and atheists who have found on *YouTube* a new virtual space to fight against hostility targeting them. These include the Egyptian Hamed Abdel Samad (*Hamed.TV*) who resides in Germany, Syrian Kosay Betar who lives in Europe and Adam Elmasri who resides in Australia (Elsässer, 2021). They broadcast from the West because critics of Islam usually face punishment in the Arab region. For instance, the Egyptian student Karim al-Banna was sentenced to three years in prison in 2015, for disclosing his atheism on *Facebook*. Also, the Egyptian journalist Fatima Naoot was sentenced to three years in prison in 2016 for criticising the sacrificing of animals for an Islamic feast (Fathy, 2018, p. 110).

Like the UAE, the Egyptian authorities have also recently announced the decision to tax creators who earn over US$32,000 annually. This is due to the large list of 'vloggers' on *YouTube* and *TikTok*, although not all vloggers publish regularly. The decision to tax vloggers was met with scepticism by journalists such as the TV presenter Amr Adib, who questioned the extent and accuracy of the authorities' record of all vloggers and content creators online (France 24, 2021).

84 *Audiences*

There are also some social media influencers who have faced a huge backlash from followers. For instance, the two Moroccan *YouTube* influencers, Hamza and Sarah, stirred a debate on social media, after filming the funeral of their newborn daughter and posting it on *YouTube*. The clip attracted more than 730,000 views on their YouTube channel 'Sarah Hamza', which has a fan base of more than 166,000 people. The funeral clip had the 'ad' feature activated, which prompted a Moroccan media commentator to argue that the obsession with those influencers on social media has contributed to tarnishing the country's image (*Al-Arab*, 2021a, July 1). Also, the *Instagram* celebrity in Kuwait, Sondos Alqattan, came under attack after posting her criticism of the Philippine domestic workers' rights to a day off, and the retention of their passports, back in June 2018. The post followed the government's codifying these minimum standards in Kuwaiti law. Alqattan's posts went viral, and many Western cosmetics companies that had previously partnered with *Alqattan* ended their partnerships (ILO, 2021, p. 3). In Syria, a *YouTube* show came under scrutiny recently for its controversial content. With many websites and platforms (like Netflix) blocked in Syria, Syrians have flocked to *YouTube* where the number of Syrian followers exceeds those of mainstream Syrian media. A new *YouTube* series called 'NewDose', [6] an entertainment show asking people in the streets to play pranks on their friends or spouses, stirred a debate after one episode features a Syrian woman who was asked to phone her husband and claim that she had cheated on him. The husband took it seriously and, in his anger, divorced his wife; the case resulted in an outcry to end such trivial content (*Al-Arab*, 2021, Sept. 20).

Finally, other influencers can arguably be exploited as a ploy in the hands of local governments. A recent article in the *Guardian* by Michaelson and Safi (2021) argues that 20 *Instagram* influencers have been selected by Egypt's Ministry of Information to collaborate with the government as part of the new media ambassador's programme to bolster Egypt's image, and influence youth. One such *Instagram* influencer is Farida Salem, a young Egyptian athlete, who insists that her posts are not political.

Conclusion

Audience engagement can be reception-oriented or production-oriented: the former refers to audience analytics showing the metrics of sharing certain stories or the time spent on each one, while the latter refers to ways of engaging the audience to pitch story ideas or create

Audiences 85

and curate content (Nelson, 2019). The focus seems to be on metrics rather than engagement for Arab news outlets. The analytics focus more on impressions, shares, and views which, according to professionals cited in this chapter, reflect news outlets' success in seizing audiences' attention in a saturated and overly – crowded online market. Outlets, however, are not particularly interested in measuring the audience's participation in terms of engaging with the news, commenting on it, and debating the information provided by news institutions, as well as raising concerns about potential biases in such news content. Outlets do not push for content that debates critical issues pertinent to the Arab digital media sphere. This means that the monopoly of the Big Tech corporations in the digital advertising market, the need for inclusive access to the digital sphere, or privacy regulations are of little or no concern.

It is worth mentioning that the comment section in many news sites is usually deactivated, partly due to the shortage of moderators inside these outlets, especially with the rise of the so-called electronic armies, mentioned in Chapter 1. Another reason is the lack of software that can analyse posts in the Arabic language as Natural Language Processing (NLP) research in Arabic is still limited although the US dedicated some funding to Arabic NLP projects, after the 9/11 attacks (Darwish et al., 2021, pp. 74–5). There have been recent initiatives since the 2010s, however, with the launch of social media platforms and the use of social media analytics, but the main difficulty is that Arab users post in a variety of dialects or 'Arabizi' (a combination of English and Arabic) (see Ali et al., 2021, p. 127). This makes it difficult to digitally analyse the posts, due to the lack of a system capable of analysing all Arab dialects, while accounting for the complexity of Arabic morphology, orthography, and stylistics (Isani, 2020, pp. 7–8). If (Western and Arab) IT professionals were to develop systems based on the written variety or Modern Standard Arabic, they would still be faced with much orthographic inconsistency, especially on social media (Darwish et al., 2020, p. 2). This means that the representativeness of social media data in surveys from and about the region is consequently debatable because it is not possible to meaningfully measure public opinion based on sentiment analysis of individual posts, given the limited NLP measures (Isani, 2020, p. 1). Research analysing large data in Arabic language cannot be fully automated, as is the case with English-language data, although such research has become more acute post-COVID-19 with the emergence of fake news in Arabic, as will be discussed in the following chapter.

86 *Audiences*

References

Al-Arab (2021, Sept. 4) The Fake Pages Are a Headache That Haunts the Stars and Celebrities of Egypt, (in Arabic), https://bit.ly/3GtYSwV

Al-Arab (2021, Sept. 20) YouTube Programs in Syria Stir up Empty Controversy (in Arabic), https://bit.ly/34B8BEa

Al-Arab (2021a, July 1) Obsessed with Increasing Followers on YouTube at a Funeral in Morocco. Vol. 44(12106), (in Arabic), p. 18.

Al-Arab (2021b, July 1) Kuwaiti Debate Whether Residents Have the Right to Freedom of Expression. Vol. 44(12106), (in Arabic), p. 18.

Al-Ghazzi, Omar (2014) "Citizen Journalism" in the Syrian Uprising: Problematizing Western Narratives in a Local Context, *Communication Theory*, Vol. 24(4), pp. 435–54.

Ali, Ahmed, Shammur Chowdhury, Mohamed Afify, Wassim El-Hajj, Hazem Hajj, Mourad Abbas, Amir Hussein, Nada Ghneim, Mohammad Abushariah & Assal Alqudah (2021) Connecting Arabs: Bridging the Gap in Dialectal Speech Recognition, Communications of the ACM, *Special section on the Arab World*, Vol. 64(4), April 2021, pp. 124–9.

Al-Qutly, Samara (2018) Smooth but Cheap Content. *Al-Sahafa Magazine*, Vol. 3(9), Spring 2018, (in Arabic), Doha: Al Jazeera Media Institute, pp. 4–7.

Al-Zayyani, Mosaed (2021) OSN CEO: New viewers up 200%, *al-Sharq al-Awsat* (in Arabic), August 22, 2021, https://bit.ly/3yRVwQE

Arab Barometer (2018) Perceived Freedoms in the Arab World. How Do Arab Citizens Perceive Their Freedoms? https://www.arabbarometer.org/2018/10/perceived-press-freedom-freedom-of-expression-in-the-arab-world/

Ayish, Muhammad & Noha Mellor (2015) *Reporting the MENA Region*. London: Rowman & Littlefield.

Chalmers, Hanna (2019) In media We Trust? How Our Views of the Media. *IPSOS*, January 19, 2019, https://www.ipsos.com/sites/default/files/ct/publication/documents/2019-01/ipsos_views_in_media_we_trust_web.pdf

Christensen, Britt & Ali Khalil (2021) Reporting Conflict from Afar: Journalists, Social Media, Communication Technologies, and War, *Journalism Practice*, DOI: 10.1080/17512786.2021.1908839

Darwich, As-Syyid Bekhait & Haithem M. Younes (2020) Factors Influencing Public Attitudes toward Paid Online Newspaper Subscriptions- A Field Study (in Arabic), *Arab Media & Society*, Issue 30, Summer/Fall 2020, https://www.arabmediasociety.com/factors-influencing-public-attitudes-towards-paying-for-online-news-field-study-arabic/

Darwish, Kareem, Nizar Habash, Mourad Abbas, Hend Al-Khalifa, Huseein T. Al-Natsheh, Samhaa R. El-Beltagy, Houda Bouamor, Karim Bouzoubaa, Violetta Cavalli-Sforza, Wassim El-Hajj, Mustafa Jarrar & Hamdy Mubarak (2020) Panoramic Survey of Natural Language Processing in the Arab World. October 2020, https://arxiv.org/pdf/2011.12631.pdf

Dzhanova, Yelena (2021) Four Journalists Set up a Refugee-Led News Outlet in Madrid after Fleeing Syria. *Business Insider*, January 30, 2021, https://www.businessinsider.com/four-syrian-journalists-refugee-led-news-outlet-madrid-2021-6?r=US&IR=T

Ehdeed, Skina (2019) *The Emergence of Libyan Networked Publics: Social Media Use Before, During and After the Libyan Uprising.* Unpublished PhD thesis, The University of Sheffield, UK.

Elsässer, Sebastian (2021) Arab Non-believers and Freethinkers on YouTube: Re-Negotiating Intellectual and Social Boundaries, *Religions*, Vol. 12(2), https://doi.org/10.3390/rel12020106

Elswah, Mona & Philip N. Howard (2020) The Challenges of Monitoring Social Media in the Arab World: The Case of the 2019 Tunisian Elections. COMPROP DATA MEMO 2020.1, 23 MARCH, 2020.

Ernest & Young/EY (2018) Videonomics: Video Content Consumption, Production and Distribution in the MENA Region, January 2018.

Ezzat, Hanan (2020) The Making of an Egyptian Social Media Influencer, *International Journal of Innovation, Creativity and Change*, Vol. 14(11), DOI: 10.53333/IJICC2013/141108

Fathy, Noha (2018) Freedom of Expression in the Digital Age: Enhanced or Undermined? The Case of Egypt, *Journal of Cyber Policy*, Vol. 3(1), pp. 96–115, DOI: 10.1080/23738871.2018.1455884

France 24 (2021, 26 Sept) Egypt to Tax Social Media Stars, https://www.france24.com/en/live-news/20210926-egypt-to-tax-social-media-stars

Gibbs, Joseph (2020) From Peers to Professionals: Regulating Influencer Marketing in the United Arab Emirates, *Arab Media & Society* (Issue 30, Summer/Fall 2020)

Global Media Insights (2021, May 28) UAE Social Media Usage Statistics. https://www.globalmediainsight.com/blog/uae-social-media-statistics/

Haider, Abdullatif (2018) The Shaky Ethics of Citizen Journalists in Yemen, *Al-Sahafa magazine*, Vol. 3(9), Spring 2018, (in Arabic), Doha: Al Jazeera Media Institute, pp. 8–11.

Harlow, Summer & Danielle K. Kilgo (2021) Protest News and Facebook Engagement: How the Hierarchy of Social Struggle Is Rebuilt on Social Media, *Journalism & Mass Communication Quarterly*, tps://doi.org/10.1177/10776990211017243

IFEX (2021a) Egypt: Fake News and Coronavirus Trials, March 31, 2021, https://ifex.org/egypt-fake-news-and-coronavirus-trials/

ILO (2021) Promoting Balanced Media Reporting on Migrant Workers in the Arab States. ILO Brief, Beirut: ILO.

IPSOS (2017) OTT AND PREMIUM ONLINE VIDEO SERVICES IN MENA, https://www.digitalmarketingcommunity.com/researches/ott-and-premium-online-video-services-in-mena-2017-ipsos/

Isani, Mujtaba Ali (2020) Methodological Problems of Using Arabic-Language Twitter as a Gauge for Arab Attitudes Toward Politics and Society, *Contemporary Review of the Middle East*, 1–14, DOI: 10.1177/2347798920976283

88 *Audiences*

JWT Intelligence (2021) Social Media in the Middle East. *Wunderman Thompson Intelligence*, June 16, 2021, https://intelligence.wundermanthompson.com

Khalifa, Hussein, Mujeeb Saif Mohsen Al-Absy, Sherif A. Badran, Tamer M. Alkadash & Qais Ahmed Almaamari, Muskan Nagi (2020) COVID-19 Pandemic and Diffusion of Fake News through Social Media in the Arab World, *Arab Media & Society* (Issue 30, Summer/Fall 2020) https://www.arabmediasociety.com/covid-19-pandemic-and-diffusion-of-fake-news-through-social-media-in-the-arab-world/

Khalil, Joe F. & Mohamed Zayani (2021) Digitality and Debordered Spaces in the Era of Streaming: A Global South Perspective, *Television & New Media*, DOI: 10.1177/15274764211014584

Majzoub, Maya (2021) The Disabled Are the Main Absent Groups in Newsrooms, *Al-Sahafa Magazine*, Vol. 6(23), Autumn 2021, (in Arabic), Doha: Al-Jazeera Media Institute.

Michaelson, Ruth & Michael Safi (2021) Sugar-Coated Propaganda? Middle East Taps into Power of Influencers, *The Guardian*, January 29, 2021, https://www.theguardian.com/world/2021/jan/29/sugar-coated-propaganda-egypt-taps-into-power-instagram-influencers

Namous, Mohamed (2018) Destiny led them to Journalism. *Al-Sahafa Magazine*, Vol. 3(9), Spring 2018, (in Arabic), Doha: Al Jazeera Media Institute, pp. 24–9.

Nelson, Jacob (2019) The Next Media Regime; The Pursuit of 'audience engagement' in Journalism, *Journalism*, DOI: 10.1177/146-4884919862375

Onyebadi, Uche & Mohamed A. Satti (2021) Does Local News always Dominate Newspaper Front-Page News? A Study of the Kuwait Times, 2017–2019, *Journal of International and Intercultural Communication*, DOI: 10.1080/17513057.2020.1869287

Osman, Nadda (2021) Egypt: TikTok Influencers Sentenced to up to 10 years in Prison for Violating 'social values', *Middle East Eye*, June 21, 2021, https://www.middleeasteye.net/news/egypt-tiktok-influencers-sentence-prison-mawada-adham-haneen-hossam

Rizvi, Anam (2019) Dubai University Rolls out Course for 'ethical' Social Media Influencers, *The National*, October 22, 2019, https://www.thenationalnews.com/uae/education/dubai-university-rolls-out-course-for-ethical-social-media-influencers-1.926557

Shehada, Ameed (2018) Citizen as Journalist and Journalist as a Citizen, *Al-Sahafa Magazine*, Vol. 3(9), Spring 2018, (in Arabic), Doha: Al Jazeera Media Institute, pp. 30–7.

Shin Donghee, Chotiyaputta Veerisa & Zaid Bouziane (2021) The Effects of Cultural Dimensions on Algorithmic News: How Do Cultural Value Orientations Affect How People Perceive Algorithms? *Computers in Human Behavior*, DOI: 10.1016/j.chb.2021.107007

Sigma (2020) Open Sigma 2020 (in French), https://drive.google.com/file/d/1PULiqoLHXtA7DUNgnFlKO9pCeWHkuBUH/view

Sobeih, Yousra Mahmoud (2019) Social and Moral Responsibility of Citizen Journalism, *Arab Media & Communication Research*, Vol. 2019(26), July-September 2019, pp. 394–422 (in Arabic).

Twitter (n.d.) Guide to Twitter Ads Mena, https://business.twitter.com/en/resources/region/mena/twitter-ads-mena-guide.html

USAID (2020) Jordan Media Assessment. June 9, 2020, https://pdf.usaid.gov/pdf_docs/PA00WQVH.pdf

Zogby Research (2018) Middle East Public Opinion. https://foreignpolicy.com/wp-content/uploads/2018/12/8a1be-2018SBYFINALWEB.pdf

Notes

1 https://www.facebook.com/business/success/alghad-tv.
2 *Campji* is a project run in Lebanon by the Arab Resource Center for Popular Arts/AL-JANA Center in cooperation with DW Akademie and the GIZ/ZFD; see *Campji YouTube* site:https://www.youtube.com/channel/UCsgm-KKdF163-Emhi8Qnn8w/about.
3 See https://www.youtube.com/channel/UCqJNTGwKmgMCwfYDbnz514Q.
4 See http://www.youtube.com/user/EyshElly/.
5 See http://www.youtube.com/user/sa7iChannel.
6 See NewDose channel on YouTube: https://www.youtube.com/channel/UCHpsr50yB-YgIuTw4U_kptg; the channel was set up in 2018, registered in Germany and has more than 1.6 million followers.

5 COVID-19

Introduction

The COVID-19 crisis has had adverse consequences on the MENA region. It led to a collapse in oil prices, and the contraction of the region's economies by more than 5 per cent in 2020, coupled with a rise in public debt from 45 per cent of GDP in 2019 to 58 per cent in 2022 (Arezki et al., 2020, p. 1). The region also fares poorly when it comes to the Global Health Security Index and its preparedness for pandemics, whether in terms of medical workforce or response planning. Most Arab states allocate limited budgets for public health: Iraq and Egypt, for instance, each spent 5 per cent of their budgets on public health in 2017, and not all Arab countries have public health insurance (Arezki et al., 2020, pp. 3–5). The region has also been hit hard in terms of labour supply due to the spread of the pandemic among workers. This is coupled with the travel restrictions which limited the possibility of bringing in temporary expatriate workers, not to mention the negative supply of capital, materials, and logistical disruptions.

COVID-19 has presented media institutions with a paradox: on the one hand, the demand for news has increased – a common occurrence during crises – and on the other, media revenues have shrunk reflecting declining advertising income. Globally, journalists have faced layoffs, such as in the USA where journalists from ethnic minority groups being the most susceptible to dismissal (Schiffrin, Clifford & Tumiatti, 2021, p. 3). The podcasting industry meanwhile has been consolidated through acquisitions by major (USA) companies; *Spotify* acquired *Warner Bros.* and *Warner Bros. DC*, *Anchor*, and *Ringer* among others, while *NY Times* acquired *Serial Productions* (PWC, 2020, p. 13). These mega-corporations now control a large share of the global market. COVID-19 led to a fall of 8 per cent in media revenue, particularly in cinema, concerts, print media, and advertising, while *OTT* Video *Platform* (*Netflix*, *Shahid*) saw an increasing demand for their services.

DOI: 10.4324/9781003218838-6

COVID-19 91

The pandemic has had devastating consequences on news gathering and dissemination processes, not only globally, but also in the Arab media sector, particularly the print media. This chapter sheds light on these consequences and the operational challenges facing the Arab media sector such as the spread of 'fake news' at the peak of the pandemic. I begin with a brief overview of the economic losses endured by the Arab states as a direct consequence of the global pandemic.

Widening the divide

A brief by the United Nations revealed the devastating consequences of COVID-19 on the Arab region, exacerbated by decades of conflicts, wars, unemployment, poverty, and inequalities (UN, 2020). The mortality rates among the region's populations of ca. 436 million people were initially low, but, by the mid-2020s, the estimated number of infected cases and death rates became of major concern. There are no accurate statistics collected and disseminated by Arab governments and published numbers do not seem to correspond to the number of infections and deaths on the ground. The pandemic led to a sharp increase in the number of poor, rising to over 115 million, or a quarter of the Arab population; many of the poor lost their jobs due to the pandemic. The region's 55.7 million people who receive humanitarian assistance, including 26 million forcibly displaced individuals, are among the most vulnerable groups. The region's contracted economy has meant a compound loss of USD 152 billion (UN, 2020), and the need for USD 1.7 billion to remedy some of the consequences of the pandemic on these vulnerable groups.

The proxy wars in Syria, Libya, and Yemen have turned the conflicts into protracted events with no end in sight, and the devastating impact of COVID-19 has not led any of these countries to a possible political settlement. The continuing disintegration of the state in each of these countries resulted in the absence of a central authority that could control the spread of the pandemic and indications that signal the risk of these countries 'moving towards a "Somalization" scenario, meaning that the disintegration and division of the state[s] become a reality' (Ali, 2020).

The pandemic not only caused disintegration and division but also hit the region's economy very hard, especially the tourism sector, which constitutes a significant proportion of several countries' income and a source of foreign currency earnings, coupled with the drastic decline in oil demands during the peak of the pandemic. The dwindling tourism revenue led to an increase in unemployment among the youth and migrants in many Arab countries. The Arab region hosts more than 15 per cent of the global migration, particularly in the GCC states, Jordan, and Lebanon (UNDP, 2020, p. 11). The remittances sent by migrants across and outside the region fell by about 20 per cent in 2020, which added to the economic shrinkage in the region (UNDP, 2020, p. 12). The remittance inflow in Yemen was estimated to be 12.6 per cent of the GDP in 2019, dropping by more than 80 per cent during the first three months of the pandemic. Remittance inflow from the GCC states to Syria dropped to USD2 million per day – down from USD 4.4. millions per day, while in Egypt, the remittance inflow dropped by more than 13 per cent. The level of production and sales in Iraq declined during the peak months of the pandemic, and in Lebanon, small enterprises temporarily stopped production, but the problem was exacerbated by the economic and financial crises that hit Lebanon before COVID-19 (*UNDP*, 2020, p. 102). The forecast for the region is equally bleak. It is estimated that the total number of people living in poverty could rise post-COVID-19, and reach 115 million, not to mention the impact of the lack of access to education and technology (p. 14).

COVID-19 also had a negative impact on education. In the GCC states, for instance, more than one million students did not attend schools or universities, and tens of thousands of jobs were lost as a result (El-Saharty et al., 2020, p. 41). The COVID-19 pandemic accelerated the spread of digital services across the region. In Jordan, for example, the Ministry of Education and the Ministry of Digital Economy partnered with a private company to create an educational portal (*Darsak*) to provide lessons for all school children, according to the national curriculum. Other initiatives included *Rawy kids* in Egypt, and *Kitabi Book Reader* in Lebanon (ITU, 2021, p. 26).

The pandemic also exacerbated the problems facing the 110 million younger people (15–29) in the region. They already suffered structural inequalities such as limited access to services, and high unemployment (reaching 23 per cent in 2020), particularly among Arab women whose unemployment rate is double that of men (ca. 42 per cent). The youth were not only battling with the devastating effects of continuing conflicts in places such as Syria, Yemen, and Libya but now had to experience the additional problems caused by COVID-19. Even those who were in employment before the pandemic now had to confront the challenge of re-entering the job market where 85 per cent of employed youth worked in the informal sector (ESCWA, 2020). The post-pandemic job market will also demand a new set of digital skills which not all youth can obtain, especially those living in rural and underprivileged areas. Saudi Arabia consequently invested more than USD15 billion to upgrade its ICT infrastructure to address this problem (PWC, 2020).

Thus, the pandemic exacerbated social inequality and the digital divide in the region. It revealed the disparity between the well-connected who could use digital technologies to resume their business and education versus the less advantaged groups such as refugees who lacked adequate Internet access and missed out on basic education and health services. The COVID-19 crisis also increased the risk of cyberattacks and digital fraud in addition to exposure to fake news (Guermazi, 2020). Network congestion during the pandemic was a concern for many Arab states caused by the intensive use of the network, the increasing demand for video and high-bandwidth entertainment services, videoconferencing, and distance learning (Guermazi, 2020).

The pandemic also caused substantial damage to the media sector, particularly the print media, which had already been struggling to survive.

Operational challenges in the media sector

The COVID-19 crisis exacerbated the crisis faced by the Arab print media with the suspension of printing facilities and distribution operations. During crisis times (and the MENA region has had a fair share of those), citizens tend to flock to news sources, especially television and social media rather than newspapers. Moreover, many readers (especially the elderly) feared the transmission of COVID-19 via printed papers, which added to their decline, not to mention the Arab governments' deprioritising aid such as bailouts to media institutions.

The COVID-19 pandemic led to the temporary, unpaid suspension of workers in the print media sector in several Arab countries. Journalists also faced salary cuts between 20 and 50 per cent. In Jordan, wages were reduced by up to 50 per cent, while in other countries such as Lebanon, Iraq, and Algeria, thousands of journalists did not receive their salaries for many months (*ATUC*, 2020). The pandemic accelerated digitisation as the future for the industry, although this too, came with a different set of challenges. The print media in Egypt, for instance, was already suffering the consequences of its accumulated debt, and in 2019, it was rumoured that the Egyptian government had ordered the shutdown of the websites of several national newspapers to reduce costs. An official statement rebutted that story, however, and announced that it had contracted with a large cybersecurity firm

94 COVID-19

to oversee the websites of national papers such as *Al-Ahram,* after it was hacked the previous year. The debt of Egyptian state-owned print media was estimated to exceed one billion dollars in 2020 (ATUC, 2020). The Egyptian government called for the digital transformation of state-funded newspapers because of the declining newspaper readership. Egypt considered this as an inevitable and urgent matter which needed attention and had been working on new measures to speed up the disposal of newspapers that had large deficits. One measure was to stop the printing of the evening editions of state-owned newspapers in 2021 and move them online. The government also announced that it did not want to close state newspapers, but only to reduce the number of staff. One measure taken was to assign the simultaneous responsibility for two or three newspapers to one editor in order to reduce the cost of hiring new editors (*Al-Arab,* 2021 June 30). Nonetheless, some prominent Egyptian journalists did not oppose state ownership and even called for reducing private media ownership. Mohamed Al-Baz, the television presenter, endorsed the government's attempt to acquire most of the media outlets which were previously in the hands of businessmen. He made this claim after his TV talk show was suspended for a few months because he criticised an Egyptian business tycoon in 2020. The tycoon called for salaries to be cut in the private sector which had been severely affected by the COVID-19 crisis.

Most Arab governments meanwhile rushed to order newspapers and magazines to stop printing and distribution because the circulation of this print matter may help to spread the virus (*ATUC,* 2020). Newspapers in the UAE, for instance, were only printed for subscribers during the lockdown, while news services were being provided online. Thus, the pandemic arguably accelerated the digital transformation of the Arab press (Al-Shamali, 2020). The print media in Iraq was suffering a significant deterioration, with a sharp decline in the circulation of newspapers falling from 171 newspapers and magazines in 2003 to merely 21 in 2020; all of these distributed 30,000 copies per day, mainly to government and private institutions. Post-COVID-19, many newspapers publish only digital editions with fewer pages, while other newspapers reduced the wages of their staff or went bankrupt. The digital editions are usually offered free of charge which means a loss in advertising revenue (Afzaz, 2020) while the fixed costs for those print outlets remained the same. This is why Palestinian media outlets were dismayed by the insistence of some local authorities, landlords, and utility companies about collecting licence fees, rent, and utility bills during the pandemic, instead of showing solidarity during the economic challenge caused by the lockdowns. The financial restraints particularly hit non-state media, resulting in the decline of reliable news sources (*Al-Arab*, 2020 Oct 5). Newspapers in Sudan also suffered from a significant decline in circulation over the past few years. This, coupled with a sharp rise in prices, forced newspapers to raise their prices, with the subsequent decline in sales and circulation. The COVID-19 crisis and the collapse of the local currency only made the situation bleaker and the rise in transportation fees forced newspapers to be sold only in the capital, which meant losing a third of the readership and revenue (Afzaz, 2020).

The pandemic also shed light on other operational challenges such as dependency on official as well as foreign sources. A survey among a sample of Saudi citizens in Jizan (Southeast region) showed that the sample tended to rely on following the accounts of official organisations and foreign media as their main source of information about the pandemic. The media platform of the Saudi Ministry of Health on *Twitter* topped first place as the most important source of information, followed by official newspapers, and then the Saudi Press Agency (Hassan, 2021). Foreign sources were also among the most trusted: A study on a sample of thousands of *tweets* in Arabic identified the high ranking of news and information about the outbreak – particularly in the USA – followed by medical organisations. Another recent survey among a sample of Arab journalists also showed their dependency on social media to gather information during the COVID-19 pandemic (Ziani et al., 2021).

In Lebanon, the print media suffered from multiple problems, especially the financial ones that preceded the COVID-19 crisis. George Solaj, deputy head of the Press Syndicate Council, said that advertisements, the main source of income for many newspapers, had fallen dramatically in 2020 (Afzaz, 2020). Indeed, the COVID-19 crisis led to a sharp decline in advertising revenue for the print media, because the distribution of newspapers and magazines was said to aid the transmission of the virus resulting in the suspension of printing operations (Aoun, 2020). In Jordan, the two largest newspapers – *Al-Rai* and *Al-Dostour* – resorted to selling their headquarters to pay for expenses that included staff wages. *Al-Ghad* newspaper was also said to be looking for a buyer of its assets. Makram Al-Tarawneh, editor-in-chief of *Al-Ghad* newspaper, opined that the print media had been suffering economically, partially due to the rise of social media sites which had seized a large share of the news market; an additional part of the problem was the declining audience's trust in the print media, and their unwillingness to pay for a daily newspaper (cited in *Al-Arab*, 2020 Nov. 4, p. 18). The dire economic situation was compounded by the censorship of publishing and the lack of government support, although the

96 *COVID-19*

print media had been on the list of institutions most affected by the COVID-19 pandemic.

In Morocco, newspapers recorded a sharp decline in their sales over the past two years, with 58 per cent of the titles ceasing to exist because of the decline in sales of 50 per cent over seven years, and the consequent reduction in advertising revenue. The total loss of suffered by the print media during 2020 was estimated to be ca. USD10 million a month. The drop in distribution and revenue affected the country's newspapers which numbered 252 in 2018 and only 105 in 2020. According to official national statistics, the circulation figures of all newspapers did not exceed 230 thousand copies in 2017, in a country with 25 million inhabitants; by contrast, the number of permits issued to electronic newspapers had increased, reaching 1,016 by the end of September 2020. The COVID-19 pandemic accelerated the deterioration of the economic position of many newspapers which stopped printing for about two months in 2020 while making available free copies of their newspapers in PDF format. The closure of cafés and other public facilities where newspapers could be purchased and made available to customers also contributed to the decline in newspaper sales. The Moroccan government, therefore, announced its support for the print media with ca. US$20 million. This announcement stirred a debate regarding how this support package would be paid out to the newspapers, and how it could help to sort out the distribution problem (Al-Alawi, 2020).

In neighbouring Tunisia, 190 journalists lost their jobs during the pandemic. It is even claimed that some advertisers refused to pay for commercial slots in shows dedicated to discussing the virus (Al-Hamami, 2020). The Tunisian Journalists Syndicate, therefore, demanded a fair distribution of state advertising contracts among public and private outlets, as well as the cancellation of debts accumulated on radio stations.

During the pandemic, major advertisers in the region diverted most of their advertising budgets to television and digital platforms, with digital advertising revenue expected to garner more than 45 per cent of the media revenue in the Arab region by 2024 (PWC, 2020). This led to huge losses for the Arab print media. The losses during the first few months of the pandemic were estimated to exceed USD 24 million in Morocco, and in Egypt, the state-owned *Al-Ahram* newspaper stated that its advertising revenue fell by 75 per cent during the pandemic. In oil-rich countries, many newspapers had either laid off staff or reduced their wages by 50 per cent (ATUC, 2020).

Other newsrooms had to let their staff work from home. For instance, one journalist based in Dubai told me that one main lesson of the COVID-19 crisis was to train staff to interview health experts remotely from home, using their mobile phones and smart publishing tools to complete their reports online. He also mentioned that his television outlet had reduced the number of staff during the pandemic (personal communication, 5 December 2021), although other journalists denied that this was the case in their outlets. Remote work, however, was not an option available for journalists in every Arab country. It was difficult for journalists in Yemen, for instance, to work from home, and to communicate with the rest of the team because of the weak internet signals.

Moreover, there were many news institutions in the region which failed to develop professional safety guidelines for their journalists or to provide adequate equipment for remote work. The problem was exacerbated by the lack of private health insurance for those journalists and administrators in news institutions (ATUC, 2020). There is no accurate record of the number of Arab journalists infected during their professional duties or the number of those who died due to the pandemic. Only one case was recorded in Egypt of the journalist Mohamed Mounir, who became infected after he was arrested and jailed on the charge of spreading 'fake news' during his reporting for *Al-Jazeera*. He died a few days after his release (ATUC, 2020). His case stirred a debate about the exponential rise of misinformation online.

Misinformation and fact-checking

The region recorded an overall low mortality rate, which could have been due to the high proportion of younger people in the population, who were considered to have less severe symptoms of COVID-19 and low-fatality cases (UNDP, 2020, p. 22). However, not all data originating from the region was reliable and one reason behind the discrepancy between the official figures and the number of cases reported on social media sites was the fact that official data was based solely on those who were tested, and the number of tests was limited in Egypt (Alhurra, 2020). The official figures for infected cases, as well as the death rate in many Arab states, were inaccurate, forcing citizens to question the true numbers and to depend on social media sites to follow the development of the infection rate in their countries.

However, social networking platforms in the region were blamed for the circulation of rumours about the first cases suspected of being infected with the virus at the beginning of the COVID-19 crisis. A recent study (*AVAAZ*, 2020) found that *Facebook* unintentionally served as an epicentre of pandemic misinformation, based on an analysis of more

98 *COVID-19*

than 100 COVID-19-related pieces of misinformation content. A further study of a sample of 1,274 people in Bahrain, Egypt, Iraq, Jordan, Morocco, Oman, Saudi Arabia, Sudan, and the UAE revealed differences in the level of confidence in social media platforms. Respondents had more confidence in the information posted on *Twitter*, followed by *Instagram*, *YouTube*, and less confidence in *WhatsApp*, *Snapchat*, *Facebook*, and *TikTok*. During the early months of the COVID-19 pandemic, respondents pointed to *WhatsApp* as the main source of rumours related to the virus (Khalifa et al., 2020). One main concern was the spread of misinformation such as the general attribution of the outbreak to a Western conspiracy against China (Essam & Abdo, 2020).

There were numerous studies and reports which had already documented the pervasiveness of social media as one of the main news sources in the region. This posed a risk to mainstream media which had resorted to drawing on social media feed to align their agenda with the public debate; but this also posed a risk to media professionals who found fake news and rumours had inundated social media feeds, coupled with a decreasing budget for vetting and verifying this information. The coverage of the COVID-19 pandemic was one example of this pressure on mainstream media which had sought to provide accurate information (Ben Messaoud, 2020). For instance, a study of the Syrian media coverage of the pandemic, based on monitoring 154 newspapers and 136 hours of television and radio broadcasts during July 2020, revealed significant gaps in the coverage with most of the information recorded by state media institutions. The study revealed that the media could not generally obtain accurate news, especially with the inaccurate data provided by the government about the scale of the spread of the pandemic in Syria (*Syrian Centre for Media and Freedom of Expression*, 2021). The study also noted that the visual content covered the pandemic more from a political angle and less as a public health issue (*Syrian Centre for Media and Freedom of Expression*, 2021). The same tendency to politicise the pandemic and its consequences was noted in the coverage of Yemeni online media, where each faction and its affiliated media outlets blamed other groups for the inability to deal with the rising infections; the Yemeni media also resorted to conspiracy theories in representing the virus as a biological weapon that targeted the region (Al-Shami, 2021).

The spread of misinformation and fake news during the pandemic has contributed to an increase in the scale of activities of several fact-checking services in the region. There are several fact-checking and monitoring initiatives in the region, set up locally, by the state, or in collaboration with Western donors.

Observatory	Country / management	When?	Donor	Active?
Nawaat fact check https://nawaat.org/ A news initiative that ran a fact-checking campaign in 2020-2021 to shed light on the real number of cases in Tunisia. It won support from *Google News Initiative* In 2021, to introduce online loyalty payments for digital media in Tunisia, setting up a Patreon account, targeting Tunisians in the diaspora, and upgrading existing web services	Tunisia	2004 (blocked in Tunisia until 2011)	• The European Endowment for Democracy (EED) • International Media Support (IMS) • Open Society • The National Endowment for Democracy (NED) • Rosa Luxemburg Stiftung (RLS) • Google News Initiative (GNI) • Heinrich-Böll-Stiftung (HBS) • Google News Initiative	Active
Mada Centre https://www.madacenter.org	Palestine/ Palestinian Center for Development and Media Freedom (MADA), NGO	2006	• European Endowment for Democracy • UNESCO • Funds for Local Cooperation (Finland) • IFEX (formerly International Freedom of Expression Exchange)	Active
No Rumours http://norumors.net/	Saudi Arabia	2012	Undeclared (but possibly state-funded)	Active
Da Begad (Is it true?) https://dabegad.com/	Egypt (licensed by the Ministry of Internal Trade)	2013	Unidentified (but possibly state-funded)	Active

(Continued)

Observatory	Country / management	When?	Donor	Active?
Akeed https://akeed.jo/ar/	Jordan / Jordan Media Institute	2014	King Abdullah II Fund for Development	Active
Fatabyyano https://fatabyyano.net/	Jordan/pan-Arab (a limited company since 2020)	2016	Western donors including Facebook	Active
Taakkad (Verify) https://verify-sy.com/	Syria (licensed in Turkey)	2016	Unidentified media donors	Active
Akhbarmeter (News metre) https://akhbarmeter.org/	Egypt	2014 (but formal launch 2018)	Unidentified (partnering with the USAID)	Active
Saheeh Misr (Accurate Egypt) https://saheeh.news/	Egypt/company registered in the USA	2018	Unidentified	Active
Matsaddaach (Do not believe it) https://matsda2sh.com/	Egypt/pan-Arab	2018	Undeclared	Active
Moroccan Observatory for Fake News	Morocco	2018	Undeclared	Not known
Haggak Taaraf https://haggak.jo/	Jordan	2018	State-funded	Active
Falso (False) https://www.falsoo.com/ Editor-in-chief, Khaled Abu Bakr, a prominent lawyer, and former TV host; recently appointed as Advisor to the head of the Suez Canal Authority	Egypt/Al-Nahda University Beni Souif	2019	Undeclared	Inactive

Misbar https://misbar.com/	Pan-Arab	2019	Founded and owned by Baaz Inc. (Social media platform based in San Francisco). MISBAR and Baaz analyse social media trends. Linked with Nabd, a personalised Arabic news aggregator, ranked #1 news app across the MENA region (based in Dubai)	Active
iCheck https://tunisiachecknews.com/about	Tunisia	2019	The Independent High Authority for Audiovisual Communication (HAICA)	Active
Fake News Algeria https://www.facebook.com/FakenewsDZ/	Algeria	2019	Undeclared	Active
Falso Libya https://falso.ly/en/	Libya / Libyan Center for Freedom of the Press (set up in 2014)	2020	Undeclared	Active
Falso Tunisia – available only on *Facebook*: www.facebook.com/falso.tn/	Tunisia	2020	Undeclared	Inactive
Collaborates with Falso Libya *El-Khabar Moukades* (News is Sacred) https://www.facebook.com/groups/2912721662136953	Tunisia	2020	Undeclared	Active

102 COVID-19

This is in addition to fact-checking segments in national media, for instance, the Lebanese *Al-Nahar Verifies* section (https://bit.ly/3Bg04CE) is an integral part of al-*Nahar* newspaper's website. Some national broadcasters also produced short segments dedicated to fact-checking such as the Tunisian TV political show, *75 Minutes*, which included a fact-checking segment, running from 2017 to 2018 (Zamit, Kooli & Toumi, 2020, p. 7). The state radio station *Tunis International Radio Channel* (RTCI) launched a short segment in 2018 titled 'We Have Verified it for You' as part of its daily morning show. The state TV channel, *Al-Watanya TV* also hosted a fact-checking segment in June 2020, introduced by the journalists who lead 'Falso Tunisia' service (Zamit, Kooli & Toumi, 2020, p. 14). During the Presidential election campaign in 2019, the platform *Birrasmi* was launched by the Tunisian NGO 'Les Cahiers de la Liberté', and founded by Tunisians residing in France and abroad. Other platforms include *Tunisia Check News,* funded by the EU, and the *Geneva Center for Governance in the Security Field.* Also, the *Facebook* group, *The Tunisian Observatory for the Fight against Fake News*, was launched during the pandemic (Zamit, Kooli & Toumi, 2020, pp. 7–10). Qatar Computing Research Institute, based at Hamad Bin Khalifa University, also led several initiatives in the cybersecurity field, including the *MADA* system which aimed to identify malicious domains, as well as the *Tanbih* (Alert) project which was developed in collaboration with MIT in the USA. *Tanbih*'s objectives were to build a news aggregator with the aim of limiting the impact of fake news and misinformation as well as media bias via a news aggregator (Pöpper, Maniatakos & Di Pietro, 2021).

Nonetheless, false information and hate speech continued to circulate during the pandemic, mostly on Arabic-language sites prompting *Facebook* to team up with, and partially fund, the Jordan-based fact-checking outlet, *Fatabayyano*, to verify some of the false information circulating on social media sites. *Fatabayyano* launched the #*ThinkBeforeYouShare* campaign to educate users about how to detect false news. In Egypt, an AI startup, *DXwand*, launched *Ask Nameesa*, a chatbot interacting with suspected COVID-19 cases through *Facebook* or *WhatsApp*. The information shared via *Ask Nameesa* is stored in the Egyptian dialect, written in Arabic (MSA), and in English (Radcliffe & Abuhmaid, 2021, p. 56). In Syria, citizen journalists were said to have joined forces with the US-based *Truepic*, a verification platform, to curb misinformation coming out of Syria (Radcliffe & Abuhmaid, 2021, p. 60).

News about the pandemic also revealed the extent of biased coverage and prejudiced discourse. In Egypt, for instance, mainstream newspapers attributed the spread of COVID-19 to foreigners coming to Egypt, and when Qatar prevented Egyptians from temporarily entering the country without a medical certificate, *Al-Ahram* newspaper called for reciprocal action, by banning Qataris from entering Egypt (Abdel Halim, 2021, p. 63). The partisan paper, *Al-Wafd*, moreover, used terms which showed clear discrimination against immigrants such as, 'May God protect the brothers in the Gulf because of the presence of many [Southeast] Asian communities that work and live there', clearly indicating that Southeast Asia may be a source of the pandemic. Op-eds referred to China in particular, as the main source, calling the pandemic 'the great Chinese virus' (Abdel Halim, 2021, pp. 66–7). Another study in March 2020 argued that hate *tweets* about COVID-19 (mentioning China and Iran, particularly) represented the largest number of hate *tweets* in the region (Alshalan et al., 2020). Another study of 18 Arabic-language *Facebook* pages which allegedly hosted conspiracy theories and misinformation indicated that users who 'liked' those pages increased by 42 per cent between September 2020 and March 2021; those *Facebook* pages had a combined fan base that exceeded two million 'likes' in March 2021 (O'Connor & Ayad, 2021). These misinformation hubs tend to pose as independent institutions or research centres and are usually linked to other global COVID-19 misinformation sites (O'Connor & Ayad, 2021); needless to say, audiences may also share fake news for a variety of reasons such as a desire to verify whether the news was real, or sharing it deliberately to alert others to that fake news.

The spread of information and misinformation about COVID-19 on *Twitter* inspired some Arab scholars to analyse this digital output and set up a new, publicly available dataset. One example is the release of 'AraCOVID19-MF' which is a manually annotated, multi-label Arabic COVID-19 dataset, focusing on fake news and hate speech detection, and based on more than 10,000 Arabic *tweets*. The system is designed to check the *tweet*'s worthiness and actuality (Ameur & Aliane, 2021). Another dataset, *ArCOV-19* is based on 2.7 million Arabic *tweets* covering the period from January 2020 to January 2021, including the most 'retweeted' and 'liked' posts. The dataset was released with search queries and a language-independent crawler to collect the *tweets* and encourage the curation of similar datasets (Haouari et al., 2021). There is still a need for much more work to process Arabic-language digital output, posted in various dialects.

104 *COVID-19*

The COVID-19 crisis not only triggered misinformation and fake news but' also spread religious misinformation via social media platforms. A recent study (Alimardani & Elswah, 2020) revealed several cases of religious misinformation in the form of false advice drawn from scriptures attributed to Islamic teachings. Some of those who spread this misleading guidance were clerics who took advantage of the pandemic to increase their number of followers; others were promoted by users who sought to attract more followers to their social media pages. This misleading information was largely based on misinterpreting scriptures and drew on the credibility of religious authority to attract users. Such religious misinformation is harder to fact-check as it demands knowledge of Islam and Islamic teachings.

The introduction of the fact-checking initiatives has neither fully addressed the problem of misinformation on social media nor has it mitigated the legal penalties facing journalists if charged with spreading misinformation. In 2020, the Algerian authorities, for instance, passed a law criminalising the publishing of fake news, deemed to harm national security or unity or incite hate speech. The pandemic also resulted in an official backlash against professional journalists as well as citizen journalists. Experts in Jordan blamed citizen journalists for the dissemination of fake news, due to the lack of accountability for their information. One Journalism professor in Jordan noted that citizen journalists did not follow professional rules, and were therefore responsible for circulating rumours in and outside Jordan (Al-Anbat, 2020). In Egypt, during the peak months of the pandemic (between March and June 2020), the authorities held criminal investigations and detained a number of citizens, activists, doctors, and journalists accused of spreading misinformation about the pandemic (IFEX, 2021a). One of those detained was Khaled Hilmi Ghoneim, a journalist. He was arrested on the charge of sharing a *Facebook* post about a hospital neglecting COVID-19 patients. Another editor, Atef Hasballah el-Sayed, was arrested after publishing a *Facebook* post alleging the increase in the number of COVID-19 cases. He was prosecuted for spreading fake news as well as 'belonging to a terrorist group'. A lawyer, Mohsen Bahnasi, and a member of the Freedoms Committee of the Egyptian Bar Association was also arrested for publishing a *Facebook* post about the increase of COVID-19 cases (IFEX, 2021b). The Egyptian human rights activist, Sanaa Seif, was also sentenced to 18 months in prison for protesting about the overcrowded prisons which exposed prisoners like her activist brother Alaa Abdel Fattah to the risk of

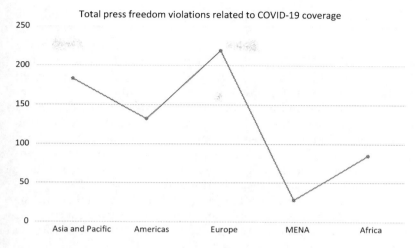

Figure 5.1 Total press violations related to COVID-19 coverage
Source: International Press Institute, https://ipi.media/covid-19-tracker-in-graphics/

contracting COVID-19. Seif was accused of disseminating false news about the deterioration of the country's health sector and the spread of the pandemic in prisons (IFEX, 2021b).

Even before the outbreak of the pandemic, the Egyptian authorities claimed that 53,000 rumours had spread in 2017 in a matter of two months, prompting the government to issue three new laws in 2018 to regulate the distribution of information online: Law No. 180/2018 about the Press and Media, Law No. 175/2018 dealing with anti-Cybercrime, and amending Law No. 58/1937 of the penal code (Sadek, 2019). The authorities suspended or blocked 500 sites in the same year – suspected of circulating fake news, and several journalists such as the editor-in-chief of *Al-Masry al-Youm*, and the editor of *Masr al-Arabiya* website were arrested for publishing false news (Sadek, 2019, p. 25).

Nonetheless, the International Press Institute (IPI) has recently published the statistics on the total press freedom violations related to COVID-19 coverage and, surprisingly, the MENA region recorded the fewest incidents.

Conclusion

The pandemic has had devastating consequences on the Arab media sector, particularly the print media, following the suspension of printing facilities and distribution operations, and the major layoff

106 *COVID-19*

of journalists across the Arab region. The COVID-19 pandemic urged Arab audiences to seek more news about the virus. This made the average reader evoke a keen interest in science, according to the editor-in-chief *of Springer Nature* in the MENA, Mohamed Yahya (cited in Abul Nasr, 2020). *Nature Arabia* journal, in fact, observed a spike in visits to its website during April and May 2020 – a 35 per cent increase – while the website of *Nature Middle East* has seen a 60 per cent increase. The crisis has also highlighted the acute need for specialised and scientific journalism, especially in the Arab region where many countries already suffer chronic diseases including non-communicable illnesses such as diabetes and chronic lung disease, not to mention the infectious liver disease – Hepatitis C virus. Due to the lack of attention to scientific journalism in the region, however, it is likely that most of the scientific journalistic content in Arab media will remain based on translations of English materials.

During the peak of the pandemic, Arab newsrooms also focused on statistics of deaths and rates of infections depending largely on medical experts and international organisations such as WHO. All newsrooms in the region in practical terms felt the lack of medical and health reporters who could simplify scientific knowledge to news audiences, and the need to develop such capacity in the future. One Arab commentator (Al-Moustafa, 2021) stated that Arab health reporting suffers from a noticeable lack of competencies, partially due to the hierarchy of specialisation in newsrooms where political, economic, and even sports news are placed higher than health reporting. Arabic-language coverage of the pandemic then aimed primarily at communicating scientific information and giving a platform for medical experts to simplify their knowledge to the general public. This aim can be described as a science literacy model where top-down communication is driven by experts, while audiences are passive consumers of this scientific knowledge (Secko, Amend & Friday, 2013, pp. 67–8). One recent initiative was to set up the Arab Network of Scientific Journalism which held a few online workshops in March and April 2021. According to its website, the network includes several academics and journalists, however, it did not seem to have held further workshops post-2021 (arabicnsj.org). The American University in Cairo (AUC) has since been offering a diploma in health reporting (https://bit.ly/3F-GwloP). These fledgling initiatives will need a few more years to yield visible results in developing health reporting and communication in the region.

References

Abdel Halim, Sohair O. (2021) The Discourse of Racism and Discrimination in the Egyptian Press at the Beginning of the Corona Crisis (in Arabic). *Arab Journal for Media and Communication Research*, Vol. 32 (Jan/March 2021), pp. 26–79.

Abul Nasr, Mona (2020) Covid-19 Puts the Focus on Scientific Journalism, *al-Sharq al-Awsat*, issue 15196, (in Arabic). July 6, 2020, https://bit.ly/3yLmx84

Afzaz, Mohamad (2020) Institutions Went Bankrupt and Revenues Stopped due to Corona, Al Jazeera.net monitors the financial conditions of the paper press in the Arab world (in Arabic). *Al-Jazeera*, May 7, 2020, https://bit.ly/2Unc6cc

Al-Alawi, Mohammed Mamouni (2020) A Sharp Decline in the Number of Newspapers in Morocco because of a Breakdown of Distribution, *Al-Arab*, Vol. 43(11871), (in Arabic), p. 18.

Al-Anbat (2020, March 2) The "Citizen Journalist" Raises more Concerns than the Coronavirus (in Arabic), https://alanbatnews.net/article/273879

Al-Arab (2020, Nov. 4) The Content and Economic Crises Lead Jordanian Newspapers to Sell Their Headquarters (in Arabic), *Al-Arab*, Vol. 43(11871), p. 18.

Al-Arab (2021, June 30) A Plan to Close or Merge Losing State-Newspapers in Egypt. Vol. 44(12105), (in Arabic), p. 18.

Al-Hamami, Al-Sadeq (2020) How Has the Corona Pandemic Changed the Press and Media Industry? (in Arabic). *Al-Jazeera Studies Center*, May 22, 2020, https://studies.aljazeera.net/ar/article/4685

Alhurra (2020, Dec. 26) The Smell of Death Is Everywhere (in Arabic), https://arbne.ws/3qD1kL7

Ali, Hassanein (2020) COVID-19 and Civil Wars in the Arab World: The Cases of Syria, Libya and Yemen, *Asian Affairs*, DOI:10.1080/03068374.2020.1837540

Alimardani, Mahsa & Mona Elswah (2020) Online Temptations: COVID-19 and Religious Misinformation in the MENA Region, *Social Media + Society*, (July-September 2020), Vol. 6(3), doi.org/10.1177/2056305120948251

Al-Moustafa, Hasan (2021) Health news and misinformation. *Al-Riyadh*, November 16, 2021, (in Arabic), https://www.alriyadh.com/1918853

Alshalan, Raghad, Al-Khalifa Hend, Alsaeed Duaa, Al-Baity Heyam, Al-shalan Shahad (2020) Detection of Hate Speech in COVID-19–Related Tweets in the Arab Region: Deep Learning and Topic Modeling Approach, *Journal of Medical Internet Research*, Vol. 22(12), DOI: 10.2196/22609

Al-Shamali, Sara (2020) Corona Dries up Newspaper Ink and Accelerates Digital Transformation (in Arabic). *Elaph*, July 12, 2020, https://elaph.com/Web/News/2020/07/1298512.html

Al-Shami, Abdulrahman M. S (2021) An Analysis of Yemeni Online Journalism Discourse on the COVID-19 Pandemic (in Arabic). *Arab Media and Society*, August 2021, https://www.arabmediasociety.com/an-analysis-of-yemeni-online-journalism-discourse-on-the-covid-19-pandemic-arabic/

108 *COVID-19*

Ameur, Mohamed Seghir Hadj & Hassina Aliane (2021) AraCOVID19-MFH: Arabic COVID-19 Multi-Label Fake News and Hate Speech Detection Dataset, arXiv:2105.03143v1 [cs.CL] May 7, 2021.

Aoun, Elie (2020) MENA Advertising Expenditure Dissected, IPSOS, May 12, 2020, https://www.ipsos.com/en-ae/mena-advertising-expendituredissected

Arezki, Rabah Moreno-Dodson, Blanca Yuting Fan, Rachel Gansey, Romeo Nguyen, Ha Nguyen, Minh Cong Mottaghi, Lili Tsakas, Constantin & Wood, Christina A. (2020) "Trading Together: Reviving the Middle East and North Africa Regional Integration in the Post-Covid Era" the Middle East and North Africa Economic Update (October), Washington, DC: World Bank. DOI: 10.1596/978-1-4648-1639-0

ATUC (2020) Effects of The Covid-19 Pandemic on Journalists and The Media Sector in the Arab World and the Middle East. *Arab Trade Union Confederation/ATUC*, December, 2020, https://www.ituc-csi.org/IMG/pdf/effects_of_covid-19_pandemic_on_journos_eng.pdf

AVAAZ (2020) How Facebook Can Flatten the Curve of the Coronavirus Infodemic, April 15, 2020, https://avaazimages.avaaz.org/facebook_coronavirus_misinformation.pdf

Ben Messaoud, Moez (2020) Social Media and the COVID-19 Pandemic: The Dilemma of Fake News Clutter vs. Social Responsibility, *Journal of Arab & Muslim Media Research*, Vol. 14(1), pp. 25–45.

El-Saharty, Sameh, Igor Kheyfets, Christopher H. Herbst & Mohamed Ihsan Ajwad (2020). *Fostering Human Capital in the Gulf Cooperation Council Countries*. International Development in Focus. Washington, DC: World Bank. DOI: 10.1596/978-1-4648-1582-9.

ESCWA (2020) Impact of Covid-19 on Young People in the Arab Region, E/ESCWA/2020/POLICY BRIEF.9, https://www.unescwa.org/publications/impact-covid-19-young-people-arab-region

Essam, Bacem A. & Muhammad S. Abdo (2020) How Do Arab Tweeters Perceive the COVID-19 Pandemic? *Journal of Psycholinguistic Research*, https://doi.org/10.1007/s10936-020-09715-6

Guermazi, Boutheina (2020) Digital Transformation in the Time of COVID-19: The Case of MENA. *World Bank Blogs*, July 29, 2020, https://blogs.worldbank.org/arabvoices/digital-transformation-time-covid-19-case-mena

Haouari, Fatima, Maram Hasanain, Reem Suwaileh & Tamer Elsayed (2021) ArCOV-19: The First Arabic COVID-19 Twitter Dataset with Propagation Networks, arXiv:2004.05861v4 [cs.CL], March 13, 2021.

Hassan, Zainab Mohamed Hamed (2021) The Effect of Official Saudi Media Platforms' Reliance on Twitter on the Knowledge and Behaviour of the Public Towards the Corona Pandemic (in Arabic), *Journal of Media Research*, Vol. 57(1), pp. 229–82.

IFEX (2021a) Egypt: Fake News and Coronavirus Trials, March 31, 2021, https://ifex.org/egypt-fake-news-and-coronavirus-trials/

IFEX (2021b) Silencing Dissent in MENA: How Authorities Are Targeting Exiles, Journalists and Prisoners of Conscience, April 11, 2021, https://

COVID-19 109

ifex.org/silencing-dissent-in-mena-how-authorities-are-targeting-exiles-journalists-and-prisoners-of-conscience/
ITU (2021) Digital Trends in the Arab States Region. Information and Communication Technology Trends and Developments in the Arab States region, 2017–2020. Geneva: International Telecommunication Union.
Khalifa, Hussein, Mujeeb Saif Mohsen Al-Absy, Sherif A. Badran, Tamer M. Alkadash, Qais Ahmed Almaamari & Muskan Nagi (2020) COVID-19 Pandemic and Diffusion of Fake News through Social Media in the Arab World, *Arab Media & Society* (Issue 30, Summer/Fall 2020) https://www.arabmediasociety.com/covid-19-pandemic-and-diffusion-of-fake-news-through-social-media-in-the-arab-world/
O'Connor, Ciarán & Moustafa Ayad (2021) MENA Monitor: Arabic COVID-19 Vaccine Misinformation Online, London: Institute for Strategic Dialogue/ISD, https://www.isdglobal.org/isd-publications/mena-monitor-arabic-covid-19-vaccine-misinformation-online/
Pöpper, Christina, Michail Maniatakos & Roberto Di Pietro (2021) Cyber Security Research in the Arab Region: A Blooming Ecosystem with Global Ambitions, *ACM*, April 2021, Vol. 64(4), pp. 96–101, https://cacm.acm.org/magazines/2021/4/251354-cyber-security-research-in-the-arab-region/fulltext
PWC (2020) Global Media Outlook 2020–2024. Pulling the Future Forward: The Entertainment and Media Industry Reconfigures amid Recovery. PWC: https://www.pwc.com/gx/en/industries/tmt/media/outlook.html
Radcliffe, Damian & Handil Abuhmaid (2021) How the Middle East Used Social Media in 2020. *New Media Academy*, https://papers.ssrn.com/sol3/papers.cfm?abstract_id=3826011
Sadek, George (2019) Egypt. Initiatives to Counter Fake News in Selected Countries. *The Law Library of Congress, Global Legal Research Directorate*, April 2019, pp. 25–8, https://www.loc.gov/law/help/fake-news/counter-fake-news.pdf
Schiffrin, Anya, Hannah Clifford & Kylie Tumiatti (2021) Saving Journalism: A Vision for the Post-Covid World. Washington DC: Konrad-Adenauer-Stiftung.
Secko, David M., Elyse Amend & Terrine Friday (2013) Four Models of Science Journalism. A Synthesis and Practical Assessment, *Journalism Practice*, Vol. 7(1), pp. 62–80.
Syrian Centre for Media & Freedom of Expression (2021) Syrian Media Coverage of the COVID-19 Pandemic. June 2021, https://scm.bz/en/en-studies/syrian-media-coverage-of-the-covid-19-pandemic-en
UN (2020) Policy Brief: The Impact of COVID-19 on the Arab Region. An Opportunity to Build Back Better. July 2020, https://unsdg.un.org/resources/policy-brief-impact-covid-19-arab-region-opportunity-build-back-better
UNDP (2020) Compounding Crises. Will COVID-19 and Lower Oil Prices Lead to a New Development Paradigm in the Arab Region? NY: UNDP.

110 *COVID-19*

Zamit, Fredj, Arwa Kooli & Ikram Toumi (2020) An examination of Tunisian fact-checking resources in the context of COVID-19, *Journal of Science and Communication*, Vol. 19(7), DOI: https://doi.org/10.22323/2.19070204

Ziani, Abdul-Karim, Mokhtar Elareshi, Mohammed Habes, Khalaf Mohammed That & Sana Ali (2021) Digital Media Usage Among Arab Journalists During Covid-19 Outbreak, in European, Asian, Middle Eastern, North African Conference on Management & Information Systems EAMMIS 2021: Artificial Intelligence Systems and the Internet of Things in the Digital Era, pp. 116–29.

Conclusion
Two-tier journalism

The discussion presented in the previous chapters has shed light on the following key developments in the Arab digital sphere.

First, the Arab region is host to several contradictions. It is often characterised by its lack of freedom of speech, and yet it has seen massive information leaks post-2011. It lacks digital talent, and yet the rate of internet use in the region is among the highest in the world. Its cyber defence is inadequate, and yet several states are involved in cyber offensive campaigns, aided by Western IT professionals. It is accused of stifling public debate, and yet it hosts well over 1,000 satellite channels appealing to Arabs inside and outside the region.

In addition, the regional political and digital rivalries have obstructed a more unified approach to articulating an Arab digital strategy. A resolution to these rivalries, although seemingly impossible at present, may curb the power of the Big Tech corporations, and compel them to accept a fairer distribution of digital advertising revenue. This digital rivalry has also resulted in 'digital nationalism' illustrated in local digital training initiatives, usually targeting Gulf nationals rather than using united strategies to upskill the massive youth populations across the whole region.

Second, social media was once credited with providing a new avenue for unprecedented, successful mobilisation that bypassed the need for physical meeting spaces and other logistical resources. However, this optimistic vision of technology as a liberating tool, which gives voice to the voiceless, which mobilises people across the globe and which faces challenges with elite discourses, has now been replaced by pessimistic views. It highlights the use of the digital sphere to ramp up disinformation campaigns, hate speech, and political polarisation. This is in addition to the challenges in regulating social media content, or controlling the dominance of certain platforms (Persily, 2019, p. 4). One consequence of the rise of digital crowds is the polarisation

DOI: 10.4324/9781003218838-7

112 *Conclusion: two-tier journalism*

of online spaces where emotion rather than reason is the norm. This phenomenon could lead to suppressing the already silent majority while affording more space to extremist voices. Thus, the louder the online voices, the more influence they exert on shaping public opinion and the political reaction that follows (DiResta, 2016).

Third, there is an intricate and unavoidable link between national and transnational perspectives when analysing Arab journalism. Examples of this link are manifested in the rise of Arabic-language media ventures in the diaspora (discussed in Chapter 3), not to mention the regional and international rivalries including the rivalry among international media outlets such as Russia's *RT* and China's *GCTV*, on the one hand, and established names such as the *CNN* or *BBC Arabic*, on the other. Each of these international players also re-organises the field by issuing its own journalism awards. The UK-based Anna Politkovskaya Award, for example, was granted to the Syrian journalist Kholoud Waleed in 2015 for her reporting in Syria, while Russia's *RT* issued the Khaled Alkhateb International Memorial Awards commemorating Alkhateb's freelancing career in Syria until his death in 2017. The prediction is that the global digital sphere will be balkanised with China harbouring ambitions not only to build its own *Firewall* but also to form alliances with selected nations and to develop a rival computer operating system (Booz Allen, 2020). Moreover, Russia is planning to isolate itself from the global (American) internet to avoid cyber-attacks and to push for developing an independent digital infrastructure for its allies such as Syria (Booz Allen, 2020, p. 7). It is also alleged that some Arab state media, such as in Egypt, have embraced Russian-style misinformation and cyber warfare to influence the situation in Libya and Sudan (Greenberg, 2019). The Egyptian state newspaper *Al-Ahram* also entered into an agreement with Russia's *Sputnik* news in 2015, turning over part of *Al-Ahram*'s platform to *Sputnik*. The future will show how the regional and global rivalry in cyberspace will not only continue to shape the Arab journalism field but also impact Western reporting on the region.

Fourth, Arab scholars (whose studies have been cited in previous chapters) still focus on the ubiquity of the internet and its consumption rather than on users' participation. The same applies to Western scholarship which, alarmingly, sidesteps the impact of the monopoly of the Big Tech corporations on the digital sphere in the Arab region. The previous chapters demonstrate that the internet is largely dominated by the USA in terms of language, infrastructure (cables, platforms, and operating systems), surveillance applications, and even news values. Arab countries have limited power over global

Conclusion: two-tier journalism 113

corporations such as *Google* or *Amazon* and it is therefore unthinkable that these companies will face any demands to change their practices or pay additional taxes in the region. This means that the offline power dynamics are mimicked in the digital sphere, not only among nations but also within the region, such as the digital divide between men and women, or between urban and rural resources, which continues in the digital sphere. There are some studies documenting the digital divide in the West (van Deursen et al., 2017, p. 453) which show the existence of a 'compound digital exclusion', meaning that those who may lack a certain digital skill may also lack other related skills alongside a 'sequential digital exclusion' in which the low level of such digital skills leads to lower engagement online and thus a low outcome for users. One can trace similar divides in the Arab region, but it is difficult to explain the situation among the Arab diaspora communities whose digital literacy is high, and yet their opportunities to access the journalism field in their host societies are low. Generally, there is an acute underrepresentation of ethnic minorities in European journalism fields such as in the UK (Thurman, Cornia & Kunert, 2016).

Fifth, the 'disruption' caused by digital technology seems to be confined to aesthetic values such as creating dynamic infographics or adopting social media metrics to record 'clickbait' news items and features. This implies a major disruption in the role of Arab journalists – from being partners in their national development to being curators of online news obsessed with 'clickbait' headlines at the expense of quality. The disruption then becomes artificial in that it does not involve new practices such as the AI-empowered solutions implemented in American outlets including the *Washington Post, Forbes*, or the *Associated Press* (Marconi, 2020). This advanced technology requires a major investment in Arabic-language natural language processing (NLP) which Big Tech corporations may be reluctant to implement and which Western media donors might not be willing to contemplate. Subsequently, the future of digital journalism in the region may either be the rise of a niche genre such as a few *VR* stories run by the well-funded pan-Arab satellite channels, or the outsourcing of digital news to IT companies lacking expertise in the journalism field (Stalph & Borges-Rey, 2018).

Indeed, the digital divide, understood in terms of digital skills, is a key factor to plug into analyses of digital technology in non-Western contexts such as the Arab region.[1] It is this inequality that should warrant the attention of journalists, scholars, and governments to interrogate the role of digital technology in maintaining the global digital divide and the hegemony of (American) Tech giants in the digital sphere. The current debate, instead, reiterates the traditional view

114 *Conclusion: two-tier journalism*

of technology as an impartial force for prosperity and liberation, while celebrating the Western/American model as the baseline for the Arab region to follow. It is not enough, for instance, to document the digital divide among journalists in the Global South versus those in the Global North in terms of access to the internet without also delving into the ways the internet is used to achieve certain outcomes such as bridging the gap between journalists in both spheres. The previous chapters have demonstrated the pre-occupation with access in terms of infrastructure, but not the way Arab journalists can benefit from digital technology to develop their information skills, control hate speech online, know about privacy settings and cyber-bullying, and develop creative content online that is not based on shallow entertainment with the sole aim of amassing followers and subscribers.

Finally, the discourse on technology as a driver for prosperity glosses over the use of technology as a driver for more consumerism and entertainment, rather than for citizen participation, genuine debates, and the development of human capital. The debate regarding the role of digital technology in the region tends to depict technology as either a harbinger of modernisation and change or a disrupter of native cultures. However, the rhetoric on technology as a path to prosperity conceals the reality of the inequality of access and usage, while naturalising this with some corporations (the Big Tech corporations) depicted as innovators and thus worthy of amassing wealth as a direct result of their innovations. Arab journalists, likewise, do not always question the problems of data deprivation, the lack of local hosting in the region, and the massive dependency on Big Tech services; they appear to be generally content with only a fraction of the digital advertising revenue. They also seem to be mostly occupied with being familiar with the newest online trends, and the newest apps, and being at the receiving end as consumers of digital technology. They consequently disregard the fact that technology is 'the result of decisions and actions made by humans, and it is then used by humans with motivations and goals' (Sadowski, 2020, p. 5). After all, those who shape the uses and regulations of this technology in the Global North are 'technocrats creating systems that shape society and govern people'; the rest of the world must follow these decisions and systems (Sadowski, 2020, p. 7).

Digital colonialism

Tech giants such as *Facebook* and *Google* are well placed to dominate the digital market with their massive resources and near-monopoly over digital platforms. More than half of all mobile applications in the

Conclusion: two-tier journalism 115

developing world are owned by *Facebook* and *Google* (Pisa & Polcari, 2019, p. 4). Big data about users in the Global North and South can be processed to infer information about each user and even make predictions about the users' political preferences. Big Tech's work in poorer countries such as *Google's C-squared* broadband project in Africa, is claimed to provide an affordable connectivity infrastructure, but it also opens up these markets for *Google* (Coleman, 2019, p. 429).

The Big Tech corporations also control the global digital advertising industry. *Google* alone can siphon user data across its various applications – from *Maps* to *Ads* and *Gmail* – and sell it back to local firms who cannot possibly develop competing technology. This means that 'those who have more and better data can create the best artificial intelligence services, which attracts more users, which gives them even more data to make the service better, and so on' (Kwet, 2019b). This is why technological progress in the Global South is now measured by the number of (American) computers available to local users, the number of internet users with access to either *Android* or *iOS* operating systems, the number of schools and households that are connected to the World Wide Web, the number of *tweets* posted during a political sit-in, or the number of STEM graduates who have been trained to operate (American) technological products. The global virtual market, largely dominated by *Google*'s *Android* and *Microsoft Windows*, controls over 76 per cent of the market share, and more than 80 per cent of the mobile operating systems, which means Tech giants have the power to block any content and to use their own algorithms to curate personalised content that informs what users get in their news feeds.

This American monopoly is arguably part of digital colonialism 'by controlling the digital ecosystem, Big Tech corporations control computer-mediated experiences, giving them direct power over political, economic, and cultural domains of life – a new form of imperial control' (Kwet, 2019a, p. 1). Digital colonialism, therefore, follows the same pattern as former imperialism. In the same way, as former colonial powers used to invest in railways and logistical infrastructure to transport raw materials to the colonisers, digital colonialists build communication infrastructures to harvest data from less advantaged countries and sell it for profit (Coleman, 2019, p. 420). While former colonialists use to promote their transportation projects as proof of their commitment to modernising the colonised territories, digital colonialists propagate digital technology as an emancipatory tool that will not only liberate the oppressed but also help professional communities in the Global South such as journalists to mimic Western professional norms.

116   *Conclusion: two-tier journalism*

The accumulated power of the Big Tech corporations also means that their investment in developing services such as Natural Language Processing in Arabic is commensurate with the revenues recorded in each market. *Facebook,* for instance, records nearly half of its revenue[2] in North America, which means that the corporation focuses its attention and investment on the American market, despite having much larger markets in terms of users, in the Global South. Although *Facebook* has the highest number of users in India (around 320 million), Indonesia (140 million), and Brazil (130 million) compared to only 190 million users in the USA, the corporation pays more attention to American regulations and American advertisers, as their spending on digital advertising far exceeds the spending of the Global South.

The digital sphere then is a manifestation of a new source of power, albeit 'at a spatio-temporal distance' (McCarthy, 2015, p. 4), with technology as another form of social control replicating offline power relations with its hierarchy and normativity, and reflecting the objectives of the empowered actors. This translates into a digital sphere divided into a tier-system where tier-one powers are shaping the structural, design, content, and networking arrangements (McCarthy, 2015, p. 98).

Two-tier journalism

These perspectives should direct scholars' and journalists' attention to the fact that the global journalistic field is also 'hierarchically positioned' (Anthias, 2012, p. 103) with those based in the Global South being placed far lower than those in the Global North who are entrusted with shaping the whole field. To help journalists in the Global South, the budgets for Western media donors have grown exponentially and are now estimated at ca. US$600 million annually, including charitable as well as official development projects (*BBC Media Action*, 2020, p. 32). Western media donors' logic in the Arab region seems to rest on perceiving journalists as individuals whose convictions can sway with targeted training, while completely overlooking that many of those journalists may follow a certain line in reporting, not because they are manipulated by official propaganda, but because they support certain groups or because of individual ideologies. It is not always clear, moreover, how Western media donors choose their beneficiaries, and how their donations can help shape the journalism field in the region by making it more accessible. There has also been a recent call to set up an international fund for

Conclusion: two-tier journalism 117

public interest media to be sponsored by global/Western media donors (*BBC Media Action*, 2020). The fund will arguably address the hitherto major concerns in developing countries such as the Arab region, while participating media organisations serve the interests of Western media donors and not those of their home countries (*BBC Media Action*, 2020, p. 33); however, it is still unclear how to address those concerns in concrete terms.

The dependency on the Global North also includes a dependency on Western journalists to define, narrate, and contextualise the problems of the Arab region. This has recently triggered a debate among Arab journalists about this dependency. One Egyptian journalist questioned the rationale of dependency on 'blue-eyed' foreign correspondents and their analysis of what is happening in Egypt and the region, instead of relying on local knowledge (al-Darini, 2015). His criticism was directed at both the *Egyptian News Agency* for doctoring a report by the *NY Times* Cairo bureau chief, David Kirkpatrick, to make it read like praise for the government, and Kirkpatrick himself for his inaccurate coverage, documented in a report by *iMedia-Ethics*. According to the *iMedia-Ethics* report, Kirkpatrick failed to interview Egyptian sources cited in his reports, over-relied on 'anonymous sources', and did not fact-check several statements (Roland Shearer, 2014). According to this report, several sources in Egypt claimed that Kirkpatrick never contacted them for confirmation of the facts about events involving them, including the Grand Mufti, the Coptic Pope, state officials, and families of victims of protest violence (Roland Shearer, 2014).

Moreover, in February 2022, the Arab and Middle Eastern Journalists Association (AMEJA) issued a statement (bit.ly/36TUuv0) condemning the 'orientalist and racist implications' of the Western coverage of the Ukrainian refugees while comparing them with Middle Eastern refugees in a way that seems to normalise the refugee crises in the Middle East. The statement refers to some examples of British and American reporters referring to Ukrainian refugees as '*relatively civilized*', '*are not looking to get away from areas in the Middle East*', and '*Europeans leaving in cars that look like ours*'. This type of naming, states AMEJA, may justify one conflict over another while entrenching Euro-centric biases.

On the other hand, there are some minority Arab journalists based in Europe who are equally frustrated. A few Arab journalists in Germany, for instance, were allegedly warned that they would lose their jobs if they criticised their German editors (Imron, 2021, pp. 46–8). The allegations refer to Arab (and non-white) journalists being

118 *Conclusion: two-tier journalism*

asked to slavishly follow the rules laid out by their German editors, although German and English-language services in the same German media institution do not work under similar restrictions. There was also an accusation that when it came to controversial and sensitive topics such as religion and racism, German editors ignored new perspectives suggested by Arab journalists, especially if these were 'contrary to stereotypes that they got used to, and so they feared losing control over the [overall] narrative' (Imron, 2021, p. 49). In December 2021, the Euro-Med Human Rights Monitor issued a statement expressing its concern about what is called 'Anti-Arab purge in German media' referring to the suspension of several Arab and Palestinian journalists in Deutsche Welle Arabic Service.[3]

One Arab journalist also questioned why placing Western journalists on a pedestal when some of them were involved in fabricating news – for instance, the German journalist Claas-Hendrik Relotius had to resign from *Der Spiegel* in 2018 after fabricating 14 news stories, including a story about two Iraqi children kidnapped by extremists, and a story about a Yemeni detainee in Guantanamo (Azzam, 2021, p. 88). Arab officials, nevertheless, deal with Western media as more worthy of their attention than their Arab counterparts, prompting Arab audiences to embrace the view that 'reliable information' is only available in Western, not Arab, media (Azzam, 2021, p. 90). Arab governments consequently overlook their responsibility to suppress free speech, with many reporters resorting to self-censorship out of fear of being targeted by their national security services (Azzam, 2021, p. 91).

There is also a lack of collaboration between Arab and Western journalists. For instance, the global investigation into the Paradise Papers (and the Panama Papers) was claimed by the International Consortium of Investigative Journalists (ICIJ) to be a collaboration with several journalists around the world, including a few journalists based in the Arab region. Upon examination of the list of those Arab journalists, one finds a few regular beneficiaries of Western media donors, as well as retired journalists such as the Jordanian Mahasen al-Emam, and the Egyptian Ali Zalat who is introduced on the ICIJ's website as a deputy editor at *Almasry Alyoum*, even though he left this position several years ago. Moreover, what was published on a couple of Arab sites, such as the Lebanese *Daraj*, was no more than a translation of what was printed in Anglo-American news media, highlighting Arab names mentioned in the Papers, while other sites[4], unaffiliated to donors, highlighted Western names. Genuine collaboration would provide an opportunity for all Arab journalists to participate by being

Conclusion: two-tier journalism 119

trained to extract and critique such leaked papers, including information concerning Western, and not only Arab, politicians and businessmen involved in such investigations such as the founder of *eBay* who also owns *Omidyar*, the largest Western media donor.

The Global North also defines the narratives for the Global South, including concepts of freedom, resistance, and surveillance. Western terms such as the 'Arab Spring' have been criticised by Arab commentators and scholars for undermining protestors' agency as if this so-called 'Spring' just happened to them, and not as a direct result of their actions. The term arguably conceals latent orientalism that lumps all Arabs into one mass and then denies them their active agency. Furthermore, it conceals the fact that Western countries were complicit in sustaining dictatorships in the region pre-2011 or during the 'Arab Winter' which is why Arabs used terms such as 'revolution' and 'uprising' to 'epitomize activism, empowerment and determination, denoting citizens who have the power to change their world and are going about that business with diligence and perseverance' (Khouri, 2011). Moreover, an analysis of American ambassadors' speeches during the 2011 uprisings tended to equate freedom and democracy with a free market and global trade as a prerequisite for progression and alignment with a global elite. In so doing, those ambassadors seemed to 'talk to and empower those with access to money as well as resource capital in their pursuit of constructing neoliberal consent' (Erol, 2021). Thus, knowledge emerging from the Global South is devalued and replaced by new mythology of 'hegemonic conceptions of innovation' (Milan & Treré, 2019, p. 324).

One solution offered by Arab scholars was to reject mimicking the West and revive Arab and Islamic identities instead, and Arabise educational curricula in states like Syria, Egypt, Algeria, and Morocco. However, English remains the language of science and technology across the region. Morocco, for instance, has seen a boom in English-language usage in the business, technology, and education sectors (Soussi, 2020). The Moroccan ministry of education sent out a circular stating that students seeking to be admitted to STEM university programmes must master English, while the British Council research team documented a link between English and employability in the IT sector in the Maghreb sub-region (Soussi, 2020, pp. 7–8). It is also notable that several British and American universities have set up branches in the region, and several British universities have additionally offered their Arab counterparts to either validate or franchise some courses. This is despite the existing divide between Arab and Western scholarship.

120 *Conclusion: two-tier journalism*

Two-tier media scholarship

Western scholars' monopoly over knowledge production is also reflected in media scholarship with journalism research being dominated by Western theories and views, particularly US views which are used as a benchmark (e.g. Steensen & Westlund, 2021, p. 114). There have been calls to de-Westernise data studies which entail understanding the specificity of the countries in the South, rather than dealing with them as one entity (Milan & Treré, 2019). However, a serious decolonisation effort will be predicated on rejecting the Western epistemic system as the only universal perspective and embracing a broader system that includes non-Western practices, values, norms, and knowledge. Western scholars who write about the digital divide in the Global South, nevertheless, seem completely oblivious to the divide in media scholarship, or the fact that the UK and the USA, are the first destinations for Arab media students who learn the Anglo-American model as the 'mainstream' model in Journalism and Media Studies. It is therefore important to remember that knowledge production is unevenly distributed around the world. Knowledge about the Arab region, for instance, stems primarily from American and European scholars, but not local scholarship. The same holds for other regions such as Southeast Asia, where knowledge and research about that region are delivered by Western scholars and not local nationals (Gerke & Evers, 2006, p. 4). Within such a hierarchy of knowledge production, several actors are placed according to their geographical and racial place. Educational and research institutions in the West, for example, are placed higher than those in the Arab region, and consequently, scholarly publishing is often controlled by Western intellectuals who have the power to decide what is and is not publishable.

One example is the International Communication Association (ICA) which is still regarded as 'a U.S.-centered enterprise', despite its recent expansion to include non-US scholars as presidents and fellows (Wiedemann & Meyen, 2016, p. 1491). Those non-US scholars who have been recognised in such leading roles came from countries closely linked to the USA, either educated at US universities or colleges, and are therefore influenced by American research traditions. The ICA's recognition and celebration of distinguished scholars also contribute to cementing the North American hegemonic position in the field. Eighty per cent of the ICA's most distinguished scholars are affiliated with US universities and the presidents and fellows who have joined the association have worked in 15 countries, with most of them being closely allied to the USA such as the UK, Australia, Canada,

Conclusion: two-tier journalism 121

Germany, Scandinavia, and Israel (Wiedemann & Meyen, 2016, p. 1494–6). The scientific recognition then follows a similar hierarchal order that is reflected in the field of politics, where the rules of the game and the benchmark are laid out by the most powerful actors in the field to evaluate all others. There are similar trends in the UK where, for instance, 'distinguished' scholars serving on decision-making institutions or national panels such as the Research Excellence Framework (REF) tend to come from the white majority rather than ethnic minority scholars. Even national committees entrusted with advising on diversity are dominated by white scholars, thus reflecting deeper structural inequalities in the field. This makes the current debate about inclusion, whether in the UK or the USA, an empty rhetoric with no tangible outcomes (Bhopal, 2017).

Generally, Arab media scholars struggle with poor visibility of their work in the international field and lack of funding and adequate research facilities. This further diminishes their ability to contribute meaningfully to global (Western) media scholarship. Arab academics also trail behind those in the Global North, and the gap between them, in terms of publication scores, is bigger in humanities and social sciences than in natural sciences. Co-authorships are also less frequent in humanities and social sciences including media and journalism (Demeter, 2019, p 41), despite the influence of American curricula, including research methodology in Arab universities. Co-authored publications typically involve either American scholars or Western Europeans, but hardly any collaboration with authors from other regions (Demeter, 2019, p. 47). The problem is exacerbated by the fact that the publishers within media and journalism disciplines are concentrated in the Global North, with half of the journals published in the USA, followed by the UK (Demeter, 2019, p. 45). This also means the importance of the English language for scholars in the Global South who wish to contribute to those journals. Indeed, scholars in developing countries such as the Arab region, face a paradox: their publishing in Western journals is one condition for obtaining academic tenure, but their chances of getting published are limited compared to their peers in English-language countries.

This means that the academic field is not a 'highly fair-and-square field of reality'; in truth, science is full of 'non-academic factors such as economy, politics, geographical position or cultural and epistemic differences' (Demeter, 2019, p. 38). Academia is therefore divided into successful countries with high publishing and patent scores versus those countries that lag behind in similar scores. They create the 'Matthew Effect' in which the richer and more successful keep

122 *Conclusion: two-tier journalism*

amassing more success, while those who are poorer and less successful become less visible; even if scholars from the 'Matthew countries' manage to publish in English-language journals, they are typically less cited than those originating from Western scholars (Demeter, 2019, p. 38.). It is as if knowledge is canonised if produced by Western scholars but discarded if produced by non-Western ones with the Global South emerging as 'the site of counter-epistemic and alternative practices' (Segura & Waisbord, 2019, p. 412).

Concluding remarks

Digital technology, similar to its predecessors, the telegraph and television, has stirred a debate about its levelling out force, and its potential to create peace and prosperity across an ever more interconnected world (Standage, 2007, p. 150). However, digital technology is not levelling out the field, as emphasised in the previous chapters. While it has provided a new platform for ordinary citizens and powerful agents to exchange views, the digital sphere has maintained the offline hierarchal forms of political, economic, and even cultural powers. As such, the digital sphere reproduces the same offline power relations.

One can argue that the digital divide in the global journalism field is manifested at several levels. It is a divide between Western and Arab journalists with varying connectivity and socio-economic opportunities in each sphere. It is also a divide between Western journalists who master several digital tools versus Arab journalists who lack understanding and appreciation of the possible benefits of using online applications, largely developed in the West. It is a divide between Western journalists who set the rules of online participation versus Arab journalists who are only passive consumers of this technology.

Western studies and commentaries about the Arab region tend to depict power as a causal relation between an all-powerful state and subordinate citizens. These analyses tend to overlook several factors: the fact that power relations cannot be analysed only at state-level, but should also be seen through the prism of regional rivalries as well as the position of Arab countries within the global economy. Thus, the local agency is often under-represented in Western scholarship. Chapter Three, for instance, showed how Egyptian journalists, including those on state television channels, rallied against the Minister of Information after he questioned the audience metrics in national media. This form of 'resistance' hardly features in contemporary analyses of Arab media. This indicates that scholarly debates have presented competing forces in the digital sphere: one that pushes for more surveillance and

Conclusion: two-tier journalism 123

control by global corporations and political powers, and another that highlights citizens' resistance, when the reality is indeed far more complex (Segura & Waisbord, 2019, p. 413).

Finally, what is needed now is to critique the myth of the information society as the harbinger of new opportunities and prosperity for the Global South, and acknowledge that this is just 'a metaphor that has been coined to hide the features of contemporary capitalism' (Bhuiyan, 2008, p. 105). This means that access to technology cannot be limited to the availability of broadband connections. The Arab region, as has been seen, is well connected but lacks a digitally skilled labour force, which is able to process and critique online information, including information emanating from the West. This can only be nurtured by training that is based on critical thinking, not mimicry, and to genuinely recognise and develop new perspectives emanating from the Global South.

References

Al-Darini, Ahmad (2015) Foreign Correspondents, Bless them, *Al-Masry al-Youm*, August 10, 2015, (in Arabic), https://www.almasryalyoum.com/editor/details/256

Anthias, Floya (2012) Transnational Mobilities, Migration Research and Intersectionality. Towards a Translocational Frame, *Nordic Journal of Migration Studies*, Vol. 2(2), pp. 102–10.

Azzam, Mohamed (2021) On being Dazzled by Western Journalists and the Need to Understand Context and Backgrounds, *Al-Sahafa Magazine*, Vol. 6(21), Spring 2021, (in Arabic), Doha: Al-Jazeera Media Institute, pp. 88–91.

BBC Media Action (2020) Enabling Media Markets to Work for Democracy. An International Fund for Public Interest Media. A Feasibility Study. https://luminategroup.com/posts/report/enabling-media-markets-to-work-for-democracy

Bhopal, Kalwant (2017) A Nearly All-White Diversity Panel? When Will Universities Start taking the Race Seriously? *The Guardian*, May 31, 2017, https://www.theguardian.com/higher-education-network/2017/may/31/a-clash-of-personalities-why-universities-mustnt-ignore-race

Bhuiyan, Abu Jafar Md. Shafiul Alam (2008) Postcolonial Subject. *International Communication Gazette*; Vol. 70(2), pp. 99–116.

Booz Allen (2020) Cybersecurity Threat Trends Outlook, https://www.boozallen.com/content/dam/boozallen_site/ccg/pdf/publications/top-9-cybersecurity-trends-for-2020.pdf

Coleman, Danielle (2019) Digital Colonialism: The 21st Century Scramble for Africa through the Extraction and Control of User Data and the Limitations of Data Protection Laws, *Michigan Journal of Race and Law*, Vol. 24. Available at: https://repository.law.umich.edu/mjrl/vol24/iss2/6

124 Conclusion: two-tier journalism

Demeter, Marton (2019) The Winner Takes It All: International Inequality in Communication and Media Studies Today, *Journalism & Mass Communication Quarterly*, Vol. 96(1), pp. 37–59.

DiResta, Renee (2016) Crowds and Technology, September 15, 2016, https://www.ribbonfarm.com/2016/09/15/crowds-and-technology/

Erol, Ali E. (2021) Delighted for a Dairy Queen in Egypt: US Foreign Policy Leadership Discourse in the Middle East during Arab Spring, *Journal of International and Intercultural Communication*, DOI: 10.1080/17513057.2021.1950198

Gerke, Solvay & Hans-Dieter Evers (2006) Globalizing Local Knowledge: Social Science Research on Southeast Asia, 1970–2000, *SOJOURN: Journal of Social Issues in Southeast Asia*, Vol. 21(1), pp. 1–21, DOI: 10.1355/sj21-1a

Greenberg, Nathaniel (2019) *How Information Warfare Shaped the Arab Spring. The Politics of Narrative in Egypt and Tunisia*. Edinburgh: Edinburgh University Press.

Imron, Bashir (2021) Freedom of the Press in Germany. The White Domination and Soft Censorship, *Al-Sahafa Magazine*, Vol. 6(21), Spring 2021, (in Arabic), Doha: Al-Jazeera Media Institute, pp. 46–51.

Khouri, Rami (2011) Arab Spring or Revolution? *The Globe*, August 18, 2011, https://www.theglobeandmail.com/opinion/arab-spring-or-revolution/article626345/

Kwet, Michael (2019a) Digital Colonialism: US Empire and the New Imperialism in the Global South, *Race & Class*, Vol. 60(4), pp. 3–26.

Kwet, Michael (2019b) Digital Colonialism Is Threatening the Global South | Science and Technology News, *al Jazeera*, March 13, 2019, https://www.aljazeera.com/opinions/2019/3/13/digital-colonialism-is-threatening-the-global-south

Marconi, Francesco (2020) *Newsmakers. Artificial Intelligence and the Future of Journalism*. NY: Columbia University Press.

McCarthy, Daniel R. (2015) *Power, Information, Technology, and International Relations Theory. The Power and Politics of US Foreign Policy and Internet*. London: Palgrave.

Milan, Stefania & Emiliano Treré (2019) Big Data from the South(s): Beyond Data Universalism. *Television & New Media*, Vol. 20(4), pp. 319–35.

Persily, Nathaniel (2019) The Internet's Challenge to Democracy: Framing the Problem and Assessing Reforms, Report to the Kofi Anan Foundation, available at: https://pacscenter.stanford.edu/publication/the-internets-challenge-to-democracy-framing-the-problem-and-assessing-reforms/

Pisa, Michael & John Polcari (2019) Governing Big Tech's Pursuit of the "Next Billion Users". CGD Policy Paper 138, Febrary, 2019, Washington DC: Center for Global Development.

Ragnedda, Massimo, Maria Laura Ruiu & Felice Addeo (2019) Measuring Digital Capital: An empirical investigation. *New Media & Society*, DOI: 10.1177/1461444819869604

Conclusion: two-tier journalism 125

Roland Shearer, Rhonda (2014) NY Times Never Called Me! Anonymous Sources, Fact Check Failures Rule in David Kirkpatrick's Egypt Reporting, imediaethics.org, December 18, 2014, https://www.imediaethics.org/ny-times-never-called-me-anonymous-sources-fact-check-failures-rule-in-egypt-analysis-reveals/

Sadowski, Jathan (2020) *Too Smart. How Digital Capitalism Is Extracting Data, Controlling Our Lives, and Taking Over the World.* Cambridge, Massachusetts: MIT Press.

Segura, María Soledad & Silvio Waisbord (2019) Between Data Capitalism and Data Citizenship, *Television & New Media*, Vol. 20(4), pp. 412–9, DOI: 10.1177/1527476419834519

Soussi, Houssine (2020) World Englishes in Multilingual Morocco. *World Englishes*, 2020, pp. 1–9, https://doi.org/10.1111/weng.12512

Stalph, Florian & Eddy Borges-Rey (2018) Data Journalism Sustainability, *Digital Journalism*, Vol. 6(8), pp. 1078–89, DOI: 10.1080/21670811.2018.1503060

Standage, Tom (2007) *The Victorian Internet.* New York: Walker & Company

Steensen, Steen & Oscar Westlund (2021) *What is Digital Journalism Studies?* London: Routledge.

Thurman, Neil, Alessio Cornia & Jessica Kunert (2016) Journalists in the UK. Oxford: Reuters institute for the Study of Journalism.

van Deursen, Alexander J. A. M., Ellen J. Helsper, Rebecca Eynon & Jan A. G. M. van Dijk (2017) The Compoundness and Sequentiality of Digital Inequality. *International Journal of Communication*, Vol. 11, pp. 452–73.

Wiedemann, Thomas & Michael Meyen (2016) Internationalization Through Americanization: The Expansion of the International Communication Association's Leadership to the World, *International Journal of Communication*, Vol. 10, pp. 1489–509.

Notes

1 The digital divide has been expanded to include different uses of the internet, and developing one's digital skills, or what is known as the 'second level' of digital divide (Ragnedda et al., 2019). There is also a third level of such a divide referring to the users' ability to materialise concrete outcomes of their digital usage and the extent of their digital capital in terms of digital competencies.

2 See https://investor.fb.com/investor-events/event-details/2020/Facebook-Q3–2020-Earnings/default.aspx

3 See https://euromedmonitor.org/en/article/4798/Anti-Arab-purge-in-German-Media-is-highly-concerning

4 Examples include https://bit.ly/3gz8gVx; https://bit.ly/3oDFwPN

Index

Note: **Bold** page numbers refer to tables and *italic* page numbers refer to figures.

Abdel Fattah, Alaa 104–5
Abdel Samad, Hamed 83
Abu Hamad, Ahmad 61
Abu Taleb, Maan 60
Adib, Amr 83
advertising market 34, 40, 44, 45, 59; digital 11, 34, 44, 49, 85; online 44
Al-Ahram 37, 40, 94, 96, 103, 112
Al-Arabiya 41–3
Al-Dostour 95
Algeria: Human Capital indicators 20; newspapers 35; online news in 39–40; web-based radio station 59
Al-Ghad 75, 95
al-Haqiqa 24
al-Hayat 22, 35, 40
Al-Jazeera 22, 23, 41, 43, 77, 97
Al-Jazeera Arabic 22, 41, 43, 77
Al-Jazeera Media Academy (JMA) 66
Al-Jazeera Network 43
Al-Khabar 35
Almasry Alyoum 118
Al-Masry al-Youm 37, 39, 54, 55, 105
Al-Mehwar TV 55
Almosafer 6
Al-Nahar 35
Al-Qabas 35, 40
Alqattan, Sondos 84
Al-Rai 95
Al-Riyadh 43, 45
al-Roya 24
Al-Safir 35

Al-Sareeh 45
Al-Sharq al-Awsat 35
Althahe, Moath 49
Al-Wafd 103
Al-Watanya TV 102
AMEJA *see* Arab and Middle Eastern Journalists Association (AMEJA)
American Commission on Freedom of the Press 54
American monopoly 115
American Tech Giants 13, 29, 44, 45, 48–9, 113
American University in Cairo (AUC) 106
Ampen, Benjamin 75
Anna Politkovskaya Award 112
'Anti-Arab purge in German media' 118
Arab and Middle Eastern Journalists Association (AMEJA) 117
Arab Development Portal (ADP) 18
Arab digital economy 16
Arab digital journalism 34–5
Arab digital strategy, regional political and digital rivalries 111
Arab fact-checking services **99–101**
Arabic language 9, 11, 54, 66, 85
Arabic-language natural language processing (NLP) 113
Arabic literature 10
Arabism 2

128 *Index*

Arab journalism: digital technology in 11; disruption in 11–12
Arab Maghreb Union 2
Arab Media Forum 29
Arab national statistics agencies 18
ArabNet 59
Arab Network of Scientific Journalism 106
Arab News 40
'The Arab Podcast' 80
Arab region 1–2; COVID-19 on (*see* COVID-19 crisis); development of online and digital media in 36; digital divide 7–9, *8*; digital journalism in 1; digital media 1, 53; digital media infrastructure in (*see* digital media infrastructure); economic development 2; technology 9–11
Arabsat 41
Arab Spring 81, 119
Arab States Broadcasting Union (ASBU) Academy 41, 66
'The Arab Tyrant Manual' 80
arabtyrantmanual.com 80
Arab Winter 119
Arab youth 5–7, *6*; Western culture on 54
Arab Youth Survey (2020) 73
'AraCOVID19-MF' 103
ar-podcast.com 80
Artificial Intelligence (AI) systems 9
Ask Nameesa 102
Aswat al-Iraq (AI) 59
Aswat Masriyya (AM) 58
'At Your Service' app 76
audiences 72, 84–5; citizen journalists 78–82; distrusting news 76–8; social media influencers 82–4; young audiences 73–5

BAE Systems 26
el-Baghdadi, Iyad 80
Bahnasi, Mohsen 104
al-Baih, Khalid 80
Al-Bashir, Omar 56
Baynana 79
Al-Baz, Mohamed 94
Belaid, Nouha 62, 63
Ben Messaoud, Moez **99–101**

Betar, Kosay 83
Big Tech corporations 1, 9, 11, 13, 48, 85, 111–16
Bishr, Yaser 43
'*Black Box*' 25

Chartbeat 63
China: *GCTV* 112; global digital economy 16; Western conspiracy against 98
citizen journalism 72, 81
citizen journalists 78–82, 102, 104
citizenship: notion of 4; UAE 21
civil wars 57, 78–9
'*CNN* effect' 40–1
collaborative investigative journalism projects 62
COVID-19 crisis 90–1, 105–6; misinformation and fact-checking 97–8, **99–101**, 102–5, *105*; negative impact on education 92; operational challenges in media sector 93–7; press violations related to *105*; widening divide 91–3
C-squared broadband project 115
Cyber Army 27–8
cyber-attacks 22, 24
cyberspace 17; regional rivalry in 22–4

Daqaeq.net 24
Daraj 59, 60, 118
data analytics 18
data journalism 62
Data Journalism Hackathon 62–3
data mining 18
Data4Women 63
Deutsche Welle Arabic Service 118
developmental journalism 54
Diab, Salah 55
digital advertising: battle for 44–8; in Kuwait 46; market in Morocco 44
digital advertising market 11, 34, 44, 49, *49*, 85
digital advertising revenue 111
digital colonialism 114–16
digital divide 7–9, *8*, 113; in Global South 120
digital economy 16
'digital farms' in Egypt 61

Index 129

digital journalism 12, 34, 62, 64; in Arab region 1; development of 36; future of 113; Western literature about 10
digital labour 7
digital media: in activism 1; consumption and production 5; development in Arab region *36*; entrepreneurs 60; Jordanians' media consumption shifted towards 5; participatory nature of 10; power of 22; young people's use of 72
digital media infrastructure 16, 28–9; Internet governance 17–18; mundane surveillance 26–8; regional rivalry in cyberspace 22–4; scarce data 18–19; stagnant human capital 19–22, *20*; state surveillance 24–6
digital media sector 18, 48
digital nationalism 111
digital sphere 7, 9, 11, 16, 18, 23, 25, 28, 61, 67, 83, 85, 111–13, 116, 122, 123
digital startups 21
digital technology 10, 17, 122; in Arab journalism 11; disruption caused by 113
digital training initiatives, journalists 65–7
DisruptAD 21
Dubai: Arab journalists based in 11; social media influencers in 82
Dubai Media City 29
Al-Dumaini, Amer 46
DXwand 102

education, spending on 21
Egypt 2; *al-Youm7* in 78; '*Black Box*' 25; Cyber Army 27; 'digital farms' in 61; *DXwand* 102; foreign funding in 59; Human Capital indicators 20; lack of data visualisation 64; mainstream newspapers in 103; misinformation in 104; print media in 93–4; social media influencers in 83
Egyptian journalists 55–6
Egyptian Journalists Syndicate 38

Egyptian News Agency 117
Egyptian newspaper 37
elaph.com 35
electronic armies 23
El-Fagr 23
Elmasri, Adam 83
El-Watan 35
El-Youm 35
English language 9, 11
entrepreneurs, journalists as 58–61
El-Eraqi, Amr 62
Euro-Med Human Rights Monitor 118
Europe: Arabic-language media ventures in 61; Arab journalists in 117; Arab migrant populations in 58; refugees 13
European Endowment for Democracy 60
EyshElly channel 82

Facebook 5, 23, 44–8, 74, 75, 79, 97, 102, 103, 114–16
fact-checking, COVID-19 crisis 97–8, **99–101**, 102–5, *105*
Fadaat Media Group 41
fake news 91; on social media 76
al-Falasi, Taim 82
Fatabayyano 102
Fatabayyanu 49
Al-Fateh, Muhammad Hizam 63
al-Fayez, Abdel Wahab 45
Federation of Arab News Agencies 3
FinFisher 26
foreign funding 59–60
Freedom of Information (FOI) 62
freedom of speech 77, 111
free services, in Arabic 74

Gaddafi, Muammar 26
Gatnash, Ahmed 80
GCC *see* Gulf Cooperation Council (GCC)
GCTV 112
Geneva Center for Governance in the Security Field 102
Germany, Arab journalists in 117–18
Ghoneim, Khaled Hilmi 104
global digital advertising industry 115
global digital economy 16

130 *Index*

Global Health Security Index 90
globalisation 1, 54
Global North 114–16, 119, 121;
   dependency on 117
Global South 9, 17, 18, 53, 114–16,
   119, 121; digital divide in 120;
   opportunities and prosperity
   for 123
Google 44, 45, 47, 48, 113–15;
   C-squared broadband project 115
Google Ads 46, 47
The Guardian 22
Gulf Cooperation Council (GCC)
   2–4, 8, 21, 28–9, 66; COVID-19
   impact on education 92; political
   rivalry among states 41
Gulf War 40, 54

Hadi, Abd Rabbo Mansour 46
al-Halabi, Fadi 79
Hassan Mushaima 26
Heikal, Osama 55–6
Hespress.com 35, 36
Hezbollah 24
Hirak protest movement 56
Hosny, Mustafa 83
Houthis 23
Human Capital Index (HCI) 6, 20

Ibrahim, Alia 59
ICA *see* International
   Communication Association (ICA)
ICIJ *see* International Consortium of
   Investigative Journalists (ICIJ)
identity politics 4–5
IKTVA scheme *see* In-Kingdom
   Total Value Add (IKTVA) scheme
iMedia-Ethics report 117
inflation, newsrooms 38–40
Information and Communication
   Technology (ICT) sector 8–9, 19
Info-times 62–3
In-Kingdom Total Value Add
   (IKTVA) scheme 3
Inkyfada 60
Instagram 5, 23, 72, 84, 98
International Communication
   Association (ICA) 120
International Consortium of
   Investigative Journalists (ICIJ) 118

International Media Academy 66
International Media Support
   (IMS) 60
Internet 7–8, *8*
Internet governance 17–18
Internet Governance Forum 17
Internet of Things (IoT) devices 7
IPSOS 44
Iraq: foreign intervention in internal
   affairs 27; Human Capital
   indicators 20; level of production
   and sales in 92; print media in 94
Iraqi Anti-Terrorism Squad Force 27
Iraq War 21, 27, 41
Islamist groups 27

Jabhat al-Nusra 58
Jordan: level of trust, new media 76;
   newspapers in 95; news websites
   in 39
journalism *see individual entries*
journalism education 64
journalists 53, 67–8; digital training
   initiatives 65–7; as entrepreneurs
   58–61; as partners in nation-
   building 53–5; professional safety
   guidelines for 97; surveillance of
   55; as technologists 61–5; trapped
   in proxy wars 55–8

Khabayahom 24
Khaled Alkhateb International
   Memorial Awards 112
Khanna, Parag 1
Kholassa 63
Kirkpatrick, David 23, 117
Kurdish movements 27
Kuwait: digital advertising in 46;
   information security in 24
Kuwaiti newspapers 35

labour market integration strategies 3
Lakis, Silvana 77
Lebanon: Arab refugees in 61;
   factionalism and institutionalised
   sectarianism 57; newspapers 35;
   news websites in 39; online media
   websites in 59; print media in 95;
   Syrian refugees in 79; traditional
   media 54–5

Index 131

L'Economiste 35
Liberté 35
Libya: media sector in 58; proxy wars in 91

Ma3azef 60
Mada Masr 60
MADA system 102
Maroc Hebdo 35
Masr al-Arabiya 105
Matthew Effect 121–2
MBC Mobile Services 73
MBC Shahid.net 73
MBC Studios 73
media sector, operational challenges in 93–7
Mekameleen TV 22, 23
Michaelson, Ruth 84
Middle East: digital sphere in 25; filtering mechanism practices 23; state surveillance 26
Middle East and North Africa (MENA) region 7; COVID-19 crisis 90; World Bank, Human Capital indicators for 19–20
Middle East Broadcasting (MBC) Academy 65–6
misinformation, COVID-19 crisis 97–8, **99–101,** 102–5, *105*
mistrust 3
mobile connectivity 7, *8*
Modern Standard Arabic 2, 85
Morocco: Human Capital indicators 20; market for digital advertising in 44; newspapers in 96; online journalists in 38, 56; online news websites in 35, 43
Morsi (President) 24
Moukalled, Diana 59, 60
Mounir, Mohamed 97
mstdfr.com 80
Mstdfr Network 80
Mubarak (President) 37
mundane surveillance 26–8
Muslim Brotherhood 27, 41, 56

Nabd Oresund 61
Naoot, Fatima 83
nation-building, journalists as partners 53–5

Natural Language Processing (NLP) 85, 116
Nature Arabia journal 106
Netflix 73, 74
'NewDose' 84
news *see* newspapers; newsrooms
newspapers 22–4, 35, 54; decline in sales 96; in Jordan 95; in Morocco 96; revenues from digital advertising 44; in Sudan 95; in UAE 94; *see also individual entries*
newsrooms 34, 62, 81; battle for digital advertising 44–8; beginning of online press 34–6, *36*; inflated circulation figures 38–40; post-2011 revolutionary media 36–8; power of satellite television 40–4
Nokia Siemens 25–6
North Africa: Arab countries in 21; mobile sector in 19
North Atlantic Treaty Organization (NATO) 58
'#No to deportation' 72
NY Times 23, 117

Obama (President) 17
Office for the Prevention of Chemical Weapons (OPCW) 57
Okaz 45
Omanisation programme 3
online advertising: market 44; revenue 44
online journalists 67; in Egypt 55; in Jordan 38; in Morocco 38, 56; social media influencers as 78
online media: development in Arab region *36*; websites 59; Yemen 98
online news: in Algeria 39–40; in Jordan 39; in Lebanon 39; websites, in Morocco 35
online press, beginning of 34–6, *36*
OPCW *see* Office for the Prevention of Chemical Weapons (OPCW)
oppression 24
Orbit Showtime Network (OSN) 73
over-the-top (OTT) 73, 74

pan-Arab news channels, web traffic for 42, *42*
pan-Arab newspapers 40

132 *Index*

pan-Arab television channels 43
pan-Arab television market 41
podcasters 80
podcasting industry 90
Political Islamist movement 56
positiveness 54
post-2011 revolutionary media 36–8
PR companies 55
Press Syndicate Council 95
print media sector: COVID-19
    impact on 93; decline of 48; in
    Egypt 93–4; in Iraq 94; in Lebanon
    95; in Tunisia 45
proxy wars 91; journalists 55–8
Pub Online 35

Qasim, Hashim 39, 55

Radi, Omar 56
Ratib, Hasan 55
9rayti.com 44
religious misinformation 104
Relotius, Claas-Hendrik 118
Reporters 66
Research Excellence Framework
    (REF) 121
Return on Investment (ROI) 75
Reuters 61
RT 112
Russia: *RT* 112; *Sputnik* 112

Sabq 43
Safi, Michael 84
Sa7i channel 82
Salem, Farida 84
Sariyya, A'seel 79
satellite television, power of 40–4
Saudi Arabia: ICT services in 19;
    newspapers 45; online news sites
    40, 43; pan-Arab television market
    41; rate of connectivity in 5;
    Twitter in 75
Saudi Digital Academy 66
Saudi Press Agency 95
Saudi Research & Media Group
    (SRG) 40
saudisation schemes 3
Saudi 24 TV 43
el-Sayed, Atef Hasballah 104
scarce data 18–19
Sigma (2020) survey 77

al-Sisi (President) 37
Sky News Arabia 42, 43
Sky News Arabia Academy 66
Skype 19
Smart media4you 44–5
Snapchat 5, 82, 98
social inequality 93
social media 111; fake news on 76;
    role of audiences 72
social media analytics 85
social media influencers 78, 82–4
social media platforms 23, 74, 82;
    level of confidence in 98; religious
    misinformation via 104
social media users 75
social networking platforms 97
social responsibility of journalism
    53–4
socio-economic divisions 3
Solaj, George 95
Sputnik 112
spying devices 26
stagnant human capital 19–22, *20*
state surveillance 24–6
Sudan: Human Capital indicators 20;
    journalists in 56; newspapers in 95
Sumaisem, Absi 81
surveillance: of journalists 55;
    mundane 26–8; state 24–6
Sykes-Picot agreement 4
Syria: civil war 57; media coverage
    of pandemic 98; proxy wars in 91;
    YouTube show in 84
Syrian Electronic Army 57
Syrian Free Army 57
Syrian refugees, in Lebanon 79

Al-Tarawneh, Makram 95
tasreeba.at 24
technologists, journalists as 61–5
technology 9–11; integration inside
    newsrooms 34
telecom investment 19
The Telegraph 24
#ThinkBeforeYouShare campaign 102
Thompson Reuters Foundation 58–9
TikTok 72, 98
Tillieux, Patrick 73
trust, in news media 76–8
Tunisia: Human Capital indicators
    20; jobs loss during pandemic 96;

Index 133

print press in 45; *75 Minutes* 102;
trust in news media 77
Tunisia Check News 102
Tunisian Association for
E-Governance 62–3
Tunisian Journalists Syndicate 96
Tunisian newspapers 45
The Tunisian Observatory for the
Fight against Fake News 102
Tunis International Radio Channel
(RTCI) 102
Twitter 23, 48, 72, 74, 75, 98, 103
Twofour54 66
two-tier journalism 116–19
two-tier media scholarship 120–2

UAE 4; digital startups in 21;
newspapers in 94
Ukrainian refugees 117
unemployment rate: Arab women 92;
journalism 64; youth 6
United Nations Development
Programme (UNDP) 2
UN's SDG Tracking Tool 18

video-on-demand (VOD) 73
vloggers 83
voice, defined as 11–12
VoIP services 19

Western journalists 61, 117, 118, 122
Western literature 10

Western media donors 47, 49, 58–60,
98, 113, 116–19
Western newsrooms 63
Western scholars 12, 120–2
Western scholarship 112, 119, 122
Western technology 10
WhatsApp 5–6, 19, 98
WikiLeaks 28, 57
World Bank, Human Capital
indicators for MENA region
19–20
World Summit on Information
Society 17

Yabiladi 35
Yahya, Mohamed 106
Yemen: citizen journalists in 79;
Human Capital indicators 20;
journalists in 97; media coverage
of pandemic 98; proxy wars in
91; remittance inflow in 92; social
media sites 46
Yemen Cyber Army 22, 28
al-Younes, Qatafa 61
young audiences 73–5
'Your Right to Know' app 76
youth bulge 5–7, *6*
youth unemployment rate *6*, 6–7
YouTube 5, 28, 48, 79, 82–4, 98

Zalat, Ali 118
al-Zalzali, Asad 79